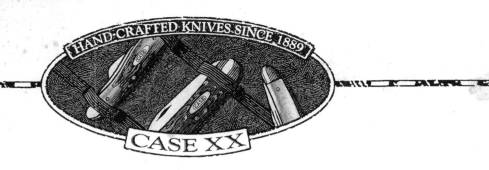

W. R. Case & Sons
Cookbook and
Historical Companion

D1510679

We do not maintain that these are original recipes.

Published by W. R. Case & Sons Cutlery Company

©Copyright 1996 W. R. Case & Sons Cutlery Company
Owens Way (P.O. Box 4000)
Bradford, Pennsylvania 16701
1-814-368-4123

Library of Congress Catalog Number: 96-092745

ISBN: 0-9653124-0-2

Designed, Edited and Manufactured by
Favorite Recipes® Press
P.O. Box 305142
Nashville, Tennessee 37230
1-800-358-0560

First Printing: 1996   12,500 copies

Book Design by Steve Newman

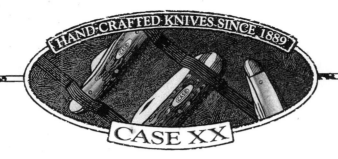

TABLE OF CONTENTS

HAND-CRAFTED KNIVES SINCE 1889

CASE XX

DEDICATION

This book is affectionately dedicated to all of you

who have proudly owned, used, and collected Case knives

through the years.

W. R. Case & Sons associates, August 5, 1996, by the Case sign in the front yard of the Owens Way facility. The Kodiak knife on the sign is the same one that used to be on the Case car.

HAND-CRAFTED KNIVES SINCE 1889

CASE XX

The Case Cutlery Recipe for Success

At W. R. Case & Sons Cutlery Company we will continually increase the value of our company through effective and ethical business practices.

We will create and maintain an environment where every associate is given the opportunity to contribute and utilize their talents to the fullest.

We will strive to expand our reputation as the industry leader in premium quality cutlery and collectibles while producing products that consistently go beyond our customers' expectations.

ACKNOWLEDGEMENTS

One of the accepted definitions of the word *acknowledge* is "to express gratitude for." The following groups and individuals have my unending gratitude.

The Associates of W. R. Case & Sons Cutlery Company.

Everyone listed as a contributor in this book should be given credit for the success of this project. It would have been impossible to do it without them. More importantly, I want to thank those associates who did not submit recipes but whose moral contributions are just as significant.

The Staff of Favorite Recipes® Press.

Their professionalism, enthusiasm, and friendship made it easier to put in the extra time and effort necessary to make this cookbook something we are proud to put the Case name on.

George T. Brinkley.

I will never forget that this was his idea. I will also never forget that he trusted my abilities enough to turn his idea into a reality.

And to you, the person reading these acknowledgements, thank you for buying our book.

Enjoy!

Joette Tripodi

April 1996

A Letter from the President

Too often companies are viewed as buildings, products, or machines. In reality, a company consists of people—ordinary folks making a living, raising families, and doing all the things that make life worthwhile.

Many of our activities seem to revolve around cooking and eating food. What we eat often says who we are. Ethnic foods, health foods, fattening foods—they all combine to define our personalities and preferences.

The idea for a Case family cookbook was conceived with two purposes in mind. First, to give our associates the opportunity to share with Case knife fans everywhere more about who we are and the things we enjoy. Secondly, to give back to our community by donating the profits from the sale of this cookbook to two local charities, Big Brothers/Big Sisters of McKean County and the McKean Literacy Team.

I hope this book brings you as much pleasure in its use as it has given us in its creation. My special thanks to all of the Case associates who shared their recipes and stories. And a very special thank you to my assistant, Joette Tripodi, whose dedicated effort and enthusiasm made this project a success.

Best Regards,

George T. Brinley

April 1996

Cookbook Contributors

Associate Name	Department/Title	Years of Service
Calvin Abrams	Shipping	26
Sharon L. Armstrong	Finishing	7
Tom Arrowsmith	Manufacturing Manager	1
Nancy Bacha	Finishing	26
Kathi Bailey	Health Services	2
Bob Baker	Assembly	4
Mike Baker	Operations Manager	7
Kenneth R. Barger	Grinding	5
Patricia Barrett	Assembly	26
Patricia L. Barrett	Finishing	1
Shirley Barrett	Etching/Engraving	30
Shirley Boser	Sales and Marketing	21
Richard Brandon	Environmental/Safety Manager	7
George T. Brinkley	President and Chief Operating Officer	5
Margaret Brocious	Finishing	27
Julie Buchanan	Etching/Engraving	20
Cindy Burritt	Customer Service	1
Jeanie Cabisca	Sales and Marketing Case Collectors Club	6
Dot Colley	Finishing	22
Bunny Comilla	Human Resources Manager	3
Martha Coverston	Accounting	2
Linda Cranmer	Grinding	23
Al Davidson	Industrial Engineering	13
Kookie Dougherty	Assembly	27
Jeanne M. DuBois	Finishing	24

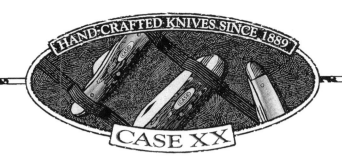

HAND-CRAFTED KNIVES SINCE 1889

CASE XX

Associate Name	Department/Title	Years of Service
Ken DuBois	Maintenance	27
Michael J. DuBois	Hafting	22
Sharon DuBois	Blanking	22
Debra R. Eddy	Controller	7
Mike Fay	Manufacturing	20
Jerome Fishkin	Case Board Member	1
Gerald Foreman	Grinding	28
Nancy Fox	Finishing	5
Staci Frantz	Accounting	1
Dave Frontino	Assembly	1
Vicki Geer	Grinding	1
Randy Gourley	Hafting	5
Lukcas Hartzell	Hafting	1
Dolores Hatch	Accounting	31
Dot Hazzard	Blanking	30
Barbara Henderson	Customer Service	6
Sharon Hollebeke	Purchasing	2
Stacey Holly	Finishing	1
Linda Huntington	Finishing	7
Ed Jessup	President, Jessup and Associates	20
E. L. "Shine" Jessup, Sr.	Retired Case Factory Representative	30+
Helen G. Johnson	Finishing	24
Kim Johnston	Finishing	5
Barbara W. Kearney	Case Board Member	1
Dick Kearney	Sales and Marketing Manager	3
Jennifer Keator	Finishing	8
Christopher Keller	Sales and Marketing	3
Jackie Kelly	Accounting	2
Steve Kellogg	Shipping	1

HAND-CRAFTED KNIVES SINCE 1889

CASE XX

Associate Name	Department/Title	Years of Service
Anne Kraft	Finishing	5
Pam Kurban	Servomation	1
Leonard Larson	Finishing	32
Dianna Lewis	Data Processing	23
Sabatina Lombardi	Assembly	30
Joseph A. Lukasiewicz	Data Processing	8
Betty L. Mack	Etching/Engraving	19
Courtney Markey	Finishing	2
Frank F. Mason	Finishing	5
Cathy McCleary	Human Resources	15
Rhoni McGraw	Assembly	1
Jane S. Moffett	Etching/Engraving	7
Judy Mosher	Customer Repair	7
Ann Nickola	Manufacturing	2
Andrew Norcross	Sales and Marketing	3
Jeanette Norris	Finishing	4
Nancy Onuffer	Finishing	3
Lisa Patry	Customer Service	1
Kevin Pipes	Owner, Smoky Mountain Knife Works	18
Nancy Price	Finishing	7
Jerry Prosser	Finishing	5
Meme Ransom	Purchasing	17
Gail Reid	Customer Service	7
Randy Reid	Owner, Shepherd Hills Walnut	23
Pat Reiner	Accounting	5
Barbara Seeley	Blanking	1
Linda Sheridan	Etching/Engraving	21
Brenda Skaggs	Customer Repair	27
Marilyn Skillman	Etching/Engraving	7

Associate Name	Department/Title	Years of Service
Cheryl Snyder	Accounting	26
Beth Soble	Accounting	18
Bobbea Southard	Finishing	5
Sherry Southard	Customer Service	23
Erma Spaulding	Finishing	27
Karen Stebbins	Hafting	7
Mark Stormer	Maintenance	24
John Sullivan	Sales and Marketing	2
Randy Travis	Case Collector	
Joette Tripodi	Assistant to the President	1
Karen Troutman	Data Processing	22
Rosa Vigliotta	Blanking	8
Robin Walker	Etching/Engraving	23
Lyn Wertenberger	Accounting	6
Rick Whelan	Finishing	5
Donna Whitford	Blanking	30
Laura Wilson	Finishing	1
Dick Yehl	Materials Manager	3
Mildred York	Finishing	7

Retirees

Name	Year Retired	Years of Service
Fred Burns	1981	$22\frac{1}{2}$
Ted Johnson	1988	$41\frac{1}{2}$
John Lombardi	1988	34
Lois Pessia	1996	21
Mary Petro	1994	70

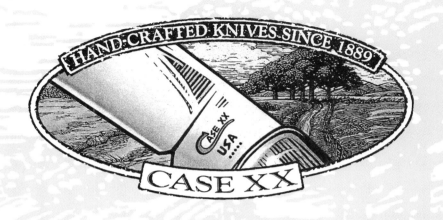

HAND-CRAFTED KNIVES SINCE 1889

CASE XX

Appetizers
&
Beverages

BREAD DIP

Meme Ransom
Purchasing
17 years

2 round loaves seedless rye
    bread
2 cups sour cream
2 cups mayonnaise
2 teaspoons celery seeds
1 teaspoon onion salt
2 teaspoons chopped parsley
2 teaspoons minced onion
4 (1-ounce) packages dried
    beef, chopped or ground

To transport this to a party, fill the bread shells with the dip and cover with their tops. Place the bread pieces in sealable plastic bags to keep them fresh.

Cut the top from each bread loaf with an electric knife. Scoop out the centers to form bread shells. Cut the bread centers into small pieces.

Mix the sour cream, mayonnaise, celery seeds, onion salt, parsley and onion in a bowl. Stir in the dried beef.

Spoon the sour cream mixture into the bread shells. Arrange on a tray surrounded by the bread pieces.

Yields 24 to 30 servings.

CHILI CON QUESO

Sharon Hollebeke
Purchasing
2 years

Sauté the onion in a nonstick skillet. Combine the cheeses in a slow cooker. Cook until the cheeses are melted. Add the picante sauce, green chiles and sautéed onion and mix well.

Fry the corn tortillas in hot oil in a skillet until golden brown, turning frequently. Drain on paper towels. Break into quarters.

Serve the chili with the chips.

Yields 18 to 20 servings.

1 onion, chopped (optional)
2 pounds Velveeta cheese, chopped
1 pound Mexican Velveeta cheese, chopped
1 jar medium picante sauce
2 cans chopped green chiles (optional)
36 corn tortillas
Vegetable oil or shortening for frying

CREAMY CHILE DIP

Patricia L. Barrett
Finishing
1 year

8 ounces cream cheese,
    softened
1 can chili with beans
1 can green chiles or jalapeño
    peppers, chopped
1 package shredded cheese
    for tacos

Layer the cream cheese, chili, green chiles and cheese in a casserole.

Bake at 350 degrees for 20 minutes or until the cheese is melted.

Serve with corn chips.

Yields 20 to 30 servings.

SHRIMP DIP

Jennifer Keator
Finishing
8 years

16 ounces cream cheese,
    softened
1 jar cocktail sauce
2 cans tiny shrimp, drained,
    rinsed

Spread the cream cheese over a platter. Spread the cocktail sauce over the cream cheese.

Top with the shrimp. Serve with your favorite butter crackers.

Yields 12 to 15 servings.

Chicken Salad Log

Kim Johnston
Finishing
5 years

Mix the cream cheese, mayonnaise, lemon juice, salt, pepper, ginger and red pepper sauce in a bowl. Stir in the chicken, eggs and 1/4 cup green onions.

Shape into a 2x8-inch log. Wrap and chill for 4 hours or until firm.

Cut the green pepper into 3 rings. Cut the rings, forming 3 strips. Arrange the strips diagonally across the chicken log, dividing the log into 4 sections.

Sprinkle 1 section with the sesame seeds, 1 with 3 tablespoons green onions, 1 with the olives and 1 with the pimento.

Serve with your favorite crackers.

Yields 12 to 20 servings.

8 ounces cream cheese, softened
1/4 cup mayonnaise or mayonnaise-type salad dressing
2 tablespoons lemon juice
1/2 teaspoon salt
1/8 teaspoon pepper
1/4 teaspoon ground ginger
4 drops of red pepper sauce
2 cups finely chopped cooked chicken
2 hard-cooked eggs, peeled, chopped
1/4 cup sliced green onions
1 green bell pepper
1 tablespoon toasted sesame seeds
3 tablespoons chopped green onions or green bell pepper
3 tablespoons chopped black olives
3 tablespoons chopped drained pimento

CLAMS CASINO

Debra R. Eddy
Controller
7 years

3 cans minced clams
$^1/_2$ cup chopped onion
$^1/_2$ cup chopped green bell
   pepper
$^1/_4$ cup chopped pimentos
$^1/_2$ tablespoon Tabasco sauce
$^1/_2$ cup Italian bread crumbs
$^1/_4$ cup melted butter

This is an excellent dish to take to a party.

Drain the clams, reserving the juice. Combine the clams, onion, green pepper, pimentos, Tabasco sauce, bread crumbs and butter in a bowl and mix well. Stir in enough of the reserved clam juice to moisten the mixture.

Spoon into a baking dish. Bake at 400 degrees for 20 to 30 minutes or until heated through.

Serve with crackers.

Yields 15 to 20 servings.

Bacon Roll-Ups

Shirley Barrett
Etching/Engraving
30 years

This came from a women's magazine I was reading at a Laundromat.

1 package pork-flavored stove-
    top stuffing mix
1 pound sliced bacon

Prepare and cook the stuffing mix using the package directions.

Cut each bacon slice into halves.

Shape 2 teaspoons of the stuffing into a ball. Wrap with 1 piece of bacon and secure with a wooden pick. Repeat until all the bacon is used.

Arrange in a single layer on a baking sheet sprayed with nonstick cooking spray.

Bake at 400 degrees for 35 to 40 minutes or until the bacon is cooked through.

Drain on paper towels. Arrange on a serving platter.

Yields 24 to 30 servings.

HAM APPETILLAS

Nancy Fox
Finishing
5 years

16 ounces cream cheese,
   softened
1/3 cup mayonnaise
2 tablespoons chopped green
   onions
1/4 cup sliced black olives
1 package extra-large flour
   tortillas, at room
   temperature
4 ounces thinly sliced ham

This recipe was in an ad for Super Bowl food. It is excellent for any party.

Mix the cream cheese, mayonnaise, green onions and olives in a bowl. Spread a thin layer over each tortilla.

Arrange the ham slices over the cream cheese mixture. Roll up tightly as for a jelly roll.

Wrap individually in plastic wrap. Chill for 3 hours to overnight. Cut into 3/4-inch slices.

For crab meat appetillas, substitute 1 can crab meat for the ham. Prepare the filling with the crab meat, 1/4 cup chopped red bell pepper, 1 cup shredded Cheddar cheese, 16 ounces softened cream cheese and 1/3 cup mayonnaise.

Yields 64 servings.

CASE XX

MUSHROOM PATTIES

Jane S. Moffett
Etching/Engraving
7 years

Combine the eggs, mushrooms, flour, bread crumbs, onion, parsley flakes and pepper in a bowl and mix well.

Shape 1/3 cup of the mushroom mixture at a time into 3 1/2-inch patties.

Heat the oil in a 10-inch skillet over medium heat. Add 4 mushroom patties at a time. Cook for 3 to 4 minutes per side or until browned.

Drain on paper towels. Keep warm in the oven.

Yields 8 servings.

3 eggs
3 cups chopped mushrooms
1/2 cup flour
1/2 cup fine dry bread crumbs
1/3 cup chopped onion
1 tablespoon dried parsley
    flakes
1/4 teaspoon pepper
3 tablespoons vegetable oil

Hot Pretzels

Patricia Barrett
Assembly
26 years

1 package ranch-style salad
    dressing mix
1 cup vegetable oil
1 teaspoon cayenne
1 teaspoon garlic salt
1¹/₄ pounds small pretzels

Combine the salad dressing mix, oil, cayenne and garlic salt in a large bowl and mix well. Add the pretzels and mix well. Spread in a roasting pan.

    Bake at 200 degrees for 2 hours, stirring frequently.

Yields 10 to 15 servings.

Sausage Ryes

Andrew Norcross
Sales and Marketing
3 years

1 package zesty sausage
8 ounces ground beef
1 pound Velveeta cheese, cut
    into cubes
2 tablespoons Worcestershire
    sauce
¹/₂ teaspoon cayenne
1 loaf party rye bread slices

Brown the sausage and ground beef separately in a large skillet, stirring until crumbly; drain.

    Combine the sausage and ground beef in a large skillet. Add the cheese gradually. Cook over low heat until the cheese is melted, stirring frequently. Add the Worcestershire sauce and cayenne. Spread the mixture generously over the bread slices. Place ¹/₂ to 1 inch apart on a lightly greased baking sheet.

    Bake at 350 to 400 degrees for 8 to 10 minutes or until lightly browned. Serve warm.

Yields 15 to 20 servings.

Vegetable Pizza

Betty L. Mack
Etching/Engraving
19 years

Unroll the crescent roll dough. Spread on an 11x15-inch baking pan, pressing to seal perforations.

Bake at 375 degrees for 11 to 13 minutes or until lightly browned. Cool completely.

Mix the cream cheese, mayonnaise and salad dressing mix in a bowl. Spread over the cooled crust.

Combine the broccoli, cauliflower, carrot, green pepper and green onions in a bowl and mix well. Sprinkle over the cream cheese mixture.

Top with the mozzarella cheese and tomatoes.

Yields 12 to 20 servings.

1 (8-count) can crescent rolls

8 ounces cream cheese, softened

$1/2$ cup mayonnaise

$1/2$ package ranch-style salad dressing mix

$3/4$ cup finely chopped fresh broccoli

$3/4$ cup finely chopped cauliflower

1 carrot, grated

$1/4$ cup finely chopped green bell pepper

1 bunch green onions, finely chopped

8 ounces mozzarella cheese, shredded

Finely chopped tomatoes

MOCK CHAMPAGNE

Jeanie Cabisca
Sales and Marketing, Case Collectors Club
6 years

1 quart apple juice, chilled
2 liters ginger ale, chilled
2 teaspoons cherry juice, or to
    taste

This is a third-generation punch recipe. Holidays would not be the same without it.

Combine the apple juice and ginger ale in a large punch bowl and mix well.

Stir in the cherry juice.

Garnish with cherries.

Yields 20 servings.

Buffers at their wheels with a combined total of 45 years of service: from right, Diana Reynolds, 7 years; Bonnie Johnson, 5 years; Mark Miller, 1 year; Lenny Larson, 32 years.

FRUIT PUNCH

Shirley Barrett
Etching/Engraving
30 years

This was served at a bridal shower for one of my very best friends. It was her mother's recipe.

Combine the ginger ale, pineapple juice, apple juice and orange juice in a large container. Chill thoroughly.

Pour into a punch bowl.

Yields 30 to 40 servings.

2 quarts ginger ale, chilled
1 (16-ounce) can pineapple juice, chilled
1 (46-ounce) can apple juice, chilled
1 (46-ounce) can orange juice, chilled

AT-HOME ORANGE JULIUS

Ann Nickola
Manufacturing
2 years

1 (6-ounce) can frozen orange
    juice concentrate
1 cup milk
1 cup water
1/2 cup sugar
1 teaspoon vanilla extract
10 to 12 ice cubes

Children love this, and it's good for them.

Combine the orange juice concentrate, milk, water, sugar, vanilla and ice cubes in a blender container. Process until slushy.

You may substitute orange-pineapple juice concentrate, pineapple juice concentrate or other flavors for the orange juice concentrate.

Yields 3 servings.

HAND-CRAFTED KNIVES SINCE 1889

CASE XX

STRAWBERRY SLUSH

Cathy McCleary
Human Resources
15 years

This will keep at least six months in the freezer. You can make one glass at a time or ten.

Combine the strawberries, sugar, lemonade concentrate, vodka and water in a large container and mix well. Freeze, tightly covered, until needed.

Spoon the desired amount into a glass. Fill with lemon-lime soda.

Yields 12 to 15 servings.

10 ounces frozen or fresh strawberries, thawed
1/2 cup sugar
1 (6-ounce) can frozen lemonade concentrate, thawed
3/4 cup vodka
1 1/2 cups water
Lemon-lime soda

HAND-CRAFTED KNIVES SINCE 1889

CASE XX

Soups, Salads
&
Breads

FIFTEEN-BEAN SOUP

Kathi Bailey
Health Services
2 years

1 package 15-bean mixed dried
   beans
1 (8-ounce) smoked picnic
   ham
1 (8-ounce) can tomato sauce
1 cup chopped onion
1 cup chopped celery
1 cup chopped carrots
3 quarts water

My sister-in-law would prepare this for our large family after an afternoon of ice skating and sleigh riding.

Rinse and sort the beans. Combine the ham, beans, tomato sauce, onion, celery, carrots and water in a large roasting pan or 5-quart casserole.

Bake, covered, at 325 degrees for 4 to 6 hours or until the ham is cooked through and the vegetables are tender.

Slice the ham and serve with the soup.

Yields 4 to 6 servings.

Brunswick Stew

George T. Brinkley
President and Chief Operating Officer
5 years

This was a favorite of my dad. He was a wonderful Southern gentleman, and when he was in the mood to cook, he could make a delicious batch of Brunswick Stew. You make it, eat some then (well, a lot) and freeze the rest for later. Brunswick Stew is very rich and hearty and in the South is usually served with barbecued pork sandwiches and coleslaw. This tastes best using the three-day method; don't try to rush it.

On the first day, place the hen and pork roast in separate large stockpots. Add enough water to cover.

Boil gently for 4 hours. Cool in the broth. Store in the refrigerator overnight.

On the second day, finely chop the hen and pork roast. Discard the skin and bones and reserve the broth.

Melt the butter in a 4-quart stockpot. Add the flour. Cook until heated through and smooth, stirring constantly. Add 2 quarts of the chicken broth and 1 quart of the pork broth gradually, stirring after each addition. Cook until slightly thickened, stirring constantly. Add the chicken, pork, onions, tomatoes, whole kernel corn, cream-style corn, salt, black pepper, red pepper, Tabasco sauce and sugar and mix well. Simmer over very low heat for 4 hours. Adjust the seasonings. Remove from the heat. Cool slightly. Store in the refrigerator overnight.

On the third day, reheat the stew over low heat until very hot, stirring frequently.

Yields 10 servings.

1 (5- to 7-pound) hen
1 (5- to 7-pound) pork roast
1/2 cup unsalted butter
1/2 cup flour
2 cups chopped onions
4 (32-ounce) cans stewed tomatoes
2 (14-ounce) cans whole kernel corn
1 (14-ounce) can cream-style corn
2 tablespoons salt, or to taste
1 tablespoon freshly ground black pepper
1 teaspoon red pepper
1 tablespoon Tabasco sauce, or to taste
1/2 cup sugar

CARROT CHEESE SOUP

Kenneth R. Barger
Grinding
5 years

3 pounds carrots, peeled,
   sliced
2 quarts water
3 cans Cheddar cheese sauce
$^1/_2$ gallon milk
1 tablespoon granulated garlic
1 cup margarine
1 cup flour
Chicken bouillon

Combine the carrots and water in a 5-quart stockpot. Simmer until tender.

Add the cheese sauce, milk and garlic and mix well.

Melt the margarine in a bowl in the microwave. Add the flour, stirring until of a paste consistency. Stir in the chicken bouillon.

Add the bouillon mixture to the stockpot. Cook until the soup is thickened and heated through, stirring frequently.

Yields 8 to 12 servings.

CHICKEN CORN SOUP

Brenda Skaggs
Customer Repair
27 years

This recipe was given to me by The Family Style Restaurant in Lancaster, Pennsylvania.

Rinse the chicken and pat dry. Bring the chicken, bouillon cubes and water to a boil in a large stockpot. Simmer for 1 hour or until the chicken is tender. Remove and debone the chicken, discarding the bones and skin. Chop the chicken and return to the stockpot.

Add the celery, onion, white pepper, 1 teaspoon salt, celery seeds, whole kernel corn, cream-style corn and celery soup and mix well. Simmer for 15 minutes or until the celery is tender.

For the dough balls, combine the flour, egg, 1/2 teaspoon salt and baking powder in a bowl and mix well. Sift through your hand into the soup, stirring constantly. Simmer for 15 minutes, stirring occasionally.

Yields 12 servings.

1 pound chicken breasts
4 chicken bouillon cubes
1 quart water
1/2 cup chopped celery
1/2 cup chopped onion
1/2 teaspoon white pepper
1 teaspoon salt
1/2 teaspoon celery seeds
1 (16-ounce) can whole kernel corn
2 (16-ounce) cans cream-style corn
1 (10-ounce) can cream of celery soup
1 cup flour
1 egg
1/2 teaspoon salt
1/4 teaspoon baking powder

Chicken Vegetable Chowder

Dick Kearney
Sales and Marketing Manager
3 years

1/2 onion, chopped (optional)
8 to 10 small red potatoes
2 cups chopped cooked chicken
1 (10-ounce) can cream of
potato soup
1 (10-ounce) can cream of
chicken soup
1 (11-ounce) can Mexicorn
1 (4-ounce) jar sliced
mushrooms
1 (4-ounce) can chopped green
chiles
1/3 cup sliced green onions
1 1/2 cups milk
1 cup chicken broth
1 1/2 cups shredded Cheddar
cheese

Sauté the onion in a nonstick skillet. Boil the unpeeled potatoes in water to cover in a saucepan until tender. Cut into bite-size pieces.

Combine the sautéed onion, potatoes, chicken, potato soup, chicken soup, Mexicorn, mushrooms, green chiles, green onions, milk and chicken broth in a Dutch oven and mix well.

Cook over medium heat for 5 to 8 minutes or until heated through. Remove from the heat.

Add the cheese, stirring until melted.

Ladle into bowls. Garnish with additional sliced green onions.

Yields 9 servings.

Cajun Clam Chowder

Jeanne M. DuBois
Finishing
24 years

Drain the clams, reserving the juice. Cook the bacon in a 4-quart stockpot until crisp. Drain, reserving 3 tablespoons drippings.

Add the potatoes, onions and celery. Sauté for 10 minutes or until tender. Sprinkle with the flour. Cook for 1 to 2 minutes or until heated through.

Add the tomatoes, bottled clam juice, water and reserved clam juice. Cook for 20 to 25 minutes or until the potatoes are tender.

Stir in the clams and hot pepper sauce. Cook for 5 to 10 minutes or until heated through.

Yields 6 servings.

1 (10-ounce) can minced baby clams
6 slices bacon, chopped
8 ounces red potatoes, chopped
2 onions, chopped
2 ribs celery, sliced
3 tablespoons flour
2 (14-ounce) cans Cajun-style stewed tomatoes
1 (8-ounce) bottle clam juice
1 cup water
1/2 to 1 teaspoon hot pepper sauce

Shortcut Potato Soup

Cindy Burritt
Customer Service
1 year

1¹/₂ cups chopped onion
¹/₄ cup butter or margarine
4 cups chopped potatoes
1 carrot, coarsely grated
2 cups water
1 teaspoon salt
¹/₂ teaspoon pepper
1 teaspoon dried dillweed
3 cups milk
2 tablespoons chopped fresh
  parsley
Frozen peas or broccoli
  (optional)
¹/₄ cup potato flakes

This is even better the second day.

Brown the onion in the butter or margarine in a large saucepan.

Add the potatoes, carrot, water, salt, pepper and dillweed. Cook over low heat for 45 minutes or until creamy.

Stir in the milk, parsley and peas. Cook until heated through. Stir in the potato flakes.

Yields 6 to 8 servings.

Sausage and Bean Soup

Sharon L. Armstrong
Finishing
7 years

This is very well liked, and the remainder (if you have any) freezes well for a second meal.

Bring the beans and water to a boil in a medium saucepan. Boil briskly for 2 minutes. Remove from the heat. Let stand, covered, for 1 hour.

Melt the butter in a 5- to 6-quart Dutch oven over medium heat. Add the onion, leeks, celery and carrots. Cook until the onion is tender, stirring constantly.

Add the parsley, chicken broth, undrained beans, potatoes and thyme and mix well. Bring to a boil; reduce the heat. Simmer, covered, for 2¹/2 hours or until the beans are tender.

Add the sausage. Simmer, covered, for 20 minutes. Season with salt.

This may be cooked on Low in a slow cooker for 10 hours.

Yields 4 to 6 servings.

1 cup small white beans,
    rinsed, drained
2 cups water
2 tablespoons butter or
    margarine
1 medium onion, finely
    chopped
3 leeks, sliced
2 ribs celery, sliced
2 carrots, sliced
¹/2 cup chopped parsley
1 (49-ounce) can chicken broth
2 medium potatoes, chopped
¹/4 teaspoon dried thyme leaves
1 pound Polish sausage or
    smoked bratwurst, cut into
    ¹/4-inch slices
Salt to taste

CRANBERRY SALAD

Dolores Hatch
Accounting
31 years

2 packages orange gelatin
2 cups hot water
1 (20-ounce) can whole
    cranberry sauce
1 cup cold water
1 (20-ounce) can crushed
    pineapple
1 cup chopped pecans

Dissolve the gelatin in the hot water in a large bowl.

Add the cranberry sauce, cold water and undrained pineapple. Stir in the pecans.

Pour into molds and chill until set.

Yields 12 to 15 servings.

STRAWBERRY FLUFF SALAD

Barbara Henderson
Customer Service
6 years

I made up this recipe many years ago. It is well liked.

Dissolve the gelatin in the hot water in a large bowl.

Add the cream cheese, stirring until melted. Stir in the strawberries and cold water. Chill until partially set.

Blend in the whipped topping. Chill until set.

This salad may be prepared with lime gelatin and pineapple or with orange gelatin and mandarin oranges.

Yields 12 to 15 servings.

2 small packages strawberry
  gelatin
2 cups hot water
8 ounces cream cheese,
  softened
1 (10-ounce) package frozen
  strawberries, thawed
3/4 cup cold water
8 ounces whipped topping

TWO GENERATIONS OF JESSUPS

When Ed "Shine" Jessup decided to start his own manufacturer's rep business, he had his son, young Eddie, show him homemade flash cards of all the Case knives time after time until he knew every one of them.

Such painstaking attention to detail inevitably led to the senior Jessup becoming Case's leading sales rep and a legend in knife circles. Since the Case rep before him had driven a white Cadillac, Jessup, Sr., made his rounds of Tennessee and Kentucky hardware stores and pawn shops in a white Caddy, too.

In a never-ending quest for sales, Ed would be away from home from Monday morning until after Eddie's bedtime on Friday night. Sure that so much traveling was not for him, Eddie went to work as a Tennessee legislative staff aide after college, helping formulate and administer the state budget. He loved his job. Probably no one was more surprised than he when he agreed to become a sales rep in East Tennessee—and to let his dad train him!

Ed did his usual fine work in training Eddie, so much so that now Eddie says: "Dad led the company in sales for years, but I think he first started thinking about retiring when my thirty-five counties started beating what he was selling in two states. After that, we decided to work together and really get after it!"

Today, Ed spends much of his time training other sales reps, giving them the same excellent encouragement and advice he has given his customers—and his son—over the past thirty years.

Eddie says he could maneuver through his territory much faster if he "didn't have to tell everyone how Dad is doing and how his golf game is!"

ASPARAGUS SALAD

E.L. ("Shine") Jessup, Sr.
Retired Case Factory Representative
30+ years

This recipe came from Ninth Street House, Paducah, Kentucky.

Soften the gelatin in ¹/₂ cup cold water. Bring the sugar, 1 cup water, vinegar and salt to a boil in a saucepan. Stir in the gelatin mixture. Cook until the gelatin is dissolved, stirring frequently.

Add the celery, pecans, pimento, lemon juice, asparagus and onion and mix well. Spoon into a 12x12-inch dish. Chill until set, stirring occasionally.

Yields 8 to 12 servings.

2 envelopes unflavored gelatin
¹/₂ cup cold water
1 cup sugar
1 cup water
¹/₂ cup vinegar
¹/₂ teaspoon salt
1 cup chopped celery
¹/₂ cup chopped pecans
1 small can chopped pimento,
  drained
Juice of 1 lemon
1 can asparagus, drained,
  sliced
1 teaspoon grated onion

BLT Salad

Dick Yehl
Materials Manager
3 years

1 head iceberg lettuce, torn
   into bite-size pieces
15 cherry tomatoes, cut into
   halves
6 hard-cooked eggs, peeled,
   sliced
1 small onion, sliced
1/3 cup sliced green onions
1/4 cup chopped green bell
   pepper
2 cups shredded Cheddar
   cheese
1 cup mayonnaise
1/2 cup milk
1/2 cup grated Parmesan
   cheese
1 teaspoon tarragon
6 slices bacon, crisp-fried,
   crumbled

This is a cool salad for a hot summer day.

Layer half the lettuce, the tomatoes, eggs, onion, green onions, green pepper and remaining lettuce in a large bowl. Top with the Cheddar cheese.

Combine the mayonnaise, milk, Parmesan cheese and tarragon in a small bowl and mix well. Pour over the salad.

Cover and chill overnight. Toss well and sprinkle with the bacon before serving.

Yields 12 servings.

NANCY'S AUNT MARY'S BEAN SALAD

Joette Tripodi
Assistant to the President
1 year

This recipe comes from a good friend of mine who, like the title says, got it from her Aunt Mary.

Combine the beans in a large bowl and mix well. Stir in the undrained artichoke hearts and undrained mushrooms. Add the green onions and olives.

Combine the wine vinegar, olive oil, garlic, parsley, oregano, salt and pepper in a medium bowl and mix well. Pour over the salad.

Cover and marinate in the refrigerator overnight.

This will keep for several days.

Yields 8 to 12 servings.

1 (15-ounce) can green beans, drained

1 (15-ounce) can yellow wax beans, drained

1 (14-ounce) can artichoke hearts, cut into quarters

2 (7-ounce) cans button mushrooms

2 green onions or 1 small purple onion, sliced

12 (or more) pimento-stuffed olives, sliced

1/3 cup wine vinegar

1/3 cup olive oil

1 clove of garlic, minced

1 tablespoon parsley

1 teaspoon oregano

Salt and pepper to taste

BROCCOLI CAULIFLOWER SALAD

Anne Kraft
Finishing
5 years

1 bunch broccoli, cut into
   florets
1 head cauliflower, cut into
   florets
3/4 full-size jar mayonnaise
2 tablespoons vinegar
1/4 cup sugar
1 package shredded cheese
1 jar bacon bits

Combine the broccoli and cauliflower in a large bowl and mix well.

Mix the mayonnaise, vinegar and sugar in a medium bowl. Pour over the salad and toss well.

Sprinkle with the cheese and bacon bits.

This is best if prepared 1 day ahead.

Yields 8 to 10 servings.

SPINACH SALAD

Cathy McCleary
Human Resources
15 years

Combine the spinach, mushrooms, eggs and bacon in a large bowl and mix well.

Combine the sugar, salt, pepper, celery seeds, mustard, vinegar and corn oil in a blender container. Process until mixed. Pour over the salad just before serving.

Top with the croutons.

Yields 12 to 15 servings.

2 packages fresh spinach, rinsed, torn into bite-size pieces
1 cup sliced fresh mushrooms
6 hard-cooked eggs, peeled, coarsely chopped
6 slices bacon, crisp-fried, crumbled
2/3 cup sugar
1 teaspoon salt
1/2 teaspoon pepper
1 teaspoon celery seeds
1 tablespoon prepared mustard
1/3 cup vinegar
1 cup corn oil
Croutons

WILTED LETTUCE

Nancy Onuffer
Finishing
3 years

4 slices bacon, cut into small
    pieces
$^1/_4$ cup vinegar
2 tablespoons water
2 teaspoons sugar
$^1/_4$ teaspoon salt
$^1/_4$ teaspoon pepper
2 green onions, sliced
1 to 2 tablespoons flour
1 egg
8 to 10 cups torn leaf lettuce

*This was my grandmother's recipe, and she also used
the dressing over dandelion greens. (Dandelion
greens need to be picked before they bloom.)*

Cook the bacon in a skillet until crisp. Remove
from the heat.

Stir in the vinegar, water, sugar, salt, pepper,
green onions, flour and egg. Cook until the
mixture is slightly thickened and the sugar is
dissolved, stirring frequently.

Place the lettuce in a large bowl. Pour the
dressing over the lettuce and toss lightly.

Yields 12 to 15 servings.

MARINATED SALAD

Robin Walker
Etching/Engraving
23 years

Mix the mayonnaise with the sugar in a small bowl.

Layer the lettuce, peas, celery, onion, green pepper and mayonnaise mixture 1/2 at a time in a 9x13-inch dish.

Marinate, covered, in the refrigerator overnight.

Sprinkle with the cheese and bacon. Chill until serving time.

Yields 8 to 10 servings.

1 cup mayonnaise
1 tablespoon sugar
1 head lettuce, chopped
1 (10-ounce) package frozen
   peas
1 cup chopped celery
1 cup chopped onion
1 green bell pepper, chopped
Shredded Cheddar cheese
Crumbled crisp-fried bacon

LINGUINI SALAD

Jeanette Norris
Finishing
4 years

1 pound linguini, broken into
    2-inch pieces
3 tomatoes, chopped
1 green pepper, chopped
1 small onion, chopped
1$1/2$ cups creamy Italian salad
    dressing
2 tablespoons seasoned salt
$1/4$ cup grated Parmesan
    cheese

*My children really like this, so I make it quite often.
My sister gave me the recipe.*

Cook the linguini using the package directions; drain well.

Combine the linguini, tomatoes, green
pepper, onion, salad dressing, seasoned salt and
cheese in a large bowl and mix well.

Chill, covered, overnight.

Yields 15 to 20 servings.

TUBETTINI SALAD

Gail Reid
Customer Service
7 years

Cook the pasta to the desired degree of doneness using the package directions.

Combine with the cheeses, pepperoni, Polish sausage and salami in a large bowl and mix well. Stir in the chick-peas and salad dressing.

Chill, covered, until serving time.

Yields 25 servings.

1 pound tubettini pasta

4 (8-ounce) packages assorted
  cheeses, chopped

1 small stick pepperoni,
  chopped

1 stick Polish sausage,
  chopped

8 ounces hard salami, chopped

1 can chick-peas

1 large bottle Italian salad
  dressing

LINDA'S SALAD DRESSING

Linda Sheridan
Etching/Engraving
21 years

2 cups mayonnaise
1/2 cup buttermilk
1 tablespoon tarragon vinegar
1 (8-ounce) can tomato sauce
1 teaspoon sugar
1/2 teaspoon garlic powder

Combine the mayonnaise, buttermilk, vinegar, tomato sauce, sugar and garlic powder in a large bowl and mix well. Pour into a covered container.

Let stand for 1 hour. Shake or stir before serving.

You may use fat-free mayonnaise or mayonnaise-type salad dressing in this recipe.

Yields 2 1/2 to 3 cups.

APPLESAUCE NUT BREAD

Pam Kurban
Servomation
1 year

This was my grandmother's recipe.

Sift the flour, sugar, baking powder, baking soda, salt and cinnamon into a large bowl.

Mix the egg, applesauce, shortening and walnuts in a small bowl. Add to the flour mixture, stirring just until moistened. Pour into a nonstick 5x9-inch loaf pan.

Bake at 350 degrees for 1 hour or until the loaf tests done.

Yields 12 servings.

2 cups flour
3/4 cup sugar
1 tablespoon baking powder
1/2 teaspoon baking soda
1/2 teaspoon salt
1/2 teaspoon cinnamon
1 egg, beaten
1 cup applesauce
2 tablespoons melted
  shortening
1 cup chopped walnuts

Banana Bread

Mildred York
Finishing
7 years

1 tablespoon sugar
2 teaspoons baking powder
1 cup mashed bananas
1/2 cup finely chopped walnuts
1 1/2 cups flour

Mix the sugar and baking powder in a bowl. Stir in the bananas and walnuts. Add the flour gradually, mixing well after each addition.

Pour into a nonstick loaf pan.

Bake at 350 degrees for 30 minutes or until the loaf tests done.

Yields 10 servings.

POPPYSEED BREAD

Cheryl Snyder
Accounting
26 years

Combine the flour, salt, baking powder, sugar, eggs, milk, oil, poppyseeds, vanilla, 1¹/₂ teaspoons almond extract and butter in a large bowl and mix well.

Pour into 4 greased small loaf pans or 2 regular loaf pans.

Bake at 350 degrees for 1 hour or until the loaves test done.

Mix the confectioners' sugar with enough water to make a thin glaze. Stir in 2 to 3 drops of almond extract. Drizzle over the hot loaves.

Yields 24 servings.

3 cups flour
1¹/₂ teaspoons salt
1¹/₂ teaspoons baking powder
2¹/₄ cups sugar
3 eggs
1¹/₂ cups milk
1¹/₈ cups vegetable oil
1¹/₂ tablespoons poppyseeds
1¹/₂ teaspoons vanilla extract
1¹/₂ teaspoons almond extract
1 tablespoon melted butter
¹/₂ cup confectioners' sugar
2 to 3 drops of almond extract

CHRISTMAS DANISH KUCHEN

Al Davidson
Industrial Engineering
13 years

1 package dry yeast
1/4 cup lukewarm water
2 teaspoons sugar
4 cups sifted flour
1 tablespoon salt
3/4 cup shortening
1 cup lukewarm scalded milk
3 egg yolks
2 tablespoons flour
1/2 teaspoon cinnamon
1/4 teaspoon nutmeg
2 egg whites, beaten
1 cup chopped dates
1 cup packed brown sugar
1 cup chopped pecans

This family recipe was handed down from a favorite aunt.

For the dough, dissolve the yeast in the water. Stir in the sugar.

Mix 4 cups flour with the salt in a large bowl. Cut in the shortening until crumbly.

Stir the yeast mixture into the milk in a medium bowl. Add the egg yolks and mix well. Add to the flour mixture and beat well. Let rise in a warm place until doubled in bulk.

For the filling, mix 2 tablespoons flour, cinnamon, nutmeg, egg whites, dates, brown sugar and pecans in a medium bowl.

Divide the dough into halves. Roll each into a rectangle on a floured surface.

Spread the filling over each rectangle. Roll up as for a jelly roll. Shape each into a wreath on a nonstick baking sheet

Bake at 325 to 350 degrees until golden brown.

Spread with your favorite basic frosting. Garnish with red cherries and additional pecans.

Yields 24 servings.

Larry's Sticky Buns

Pat Reiner
Accounting
5 years

Everyone in Customer Service loves these great-tasting buns.

Mix the cake mix, flour and yeast in a large bowl. Add the hot water, stirring until blended. Cover and let rise in a warm place for 1 hour or until doubled in bulk.

Cut the dough into halves. Roll into two 12x18-inch rectangles on a lightly floured surface. Spread the rectangles with 1/2 cup butter. Sprinkle with 1/2 cup brown sugar and cinnamon.

Pat the dough lightly and roll up as for a jelly roll. Cut each roll into 12 pieces. Place in 2 greased 9x13-inch baking pans. Cover and let rise until doubled in bulk.

Bake at 375 degrees for 25 minutes.

Melt 3/4 cup butter in a saucepan. Add 1/2 cup brown sugar, corn syrup and pecans. Simmer for 10 minutes.

Invert the hot buns onto a serving plate. Spoon the brown sugar mixture over the buns.

Yields 24 servings.

1 (2-layer) package yellow cake mix
5 cups flour
2 packages dry yeast
2 1/2 cups hot water
1/2 cup butter, softened
1/2 cup packed brown sugar
1 tablespoon cinnamon
3/4 cup butter
1/2 cup packed brown sugar
1/2 cup light corn syrup
3/4 cup chopped pecans or walnuts (optional)

YEAST ROLLS

George T. Brinkley
President and Chief Operating Officer
5 years

2 packages dry yeast
1¹/4 cups warm (105- to 115-
    degree) water
4¹/2 to 5 cups flour
3 eggs, slightly beaten
¹/2 cup melted shortening
¹/2 cup sugar
2 teaspoons salt

This makes a very nice rich-tasting roll and is wonderful to keep in the refrigerator to have ready within an hour. Our family prefers a very soft "yeasty" roll, and this is the best recipe we have found for yeast rolls.

Dissolve the yeast in ¹/4 cup of the water in a 2-cup measure. Let stand for 5 minutes.

Combine the yeast mixture, remaining 1 cup water, 2 cups of the flour, eggs, shortening, sugar and salt in a large bowl. Beat with a wooden spoon for 2 minutes. Add enough of the remaining flour gradually to make a soft dough, beating well after each addition. Cover and let rise in a warm place for 1 hour.

Punch the dough down. Cover and chill for 8 hours or longer.

Punch the dough down. Invert onto a floured surface and knead 3 to 4 times. Divide the dough into halves. (At this point, you may return half the dough to the refrigerator to prepare at another time.)

Roll each portion of dough into a rectangle on a lightly floured surface. Cut with a biscuit cutter. Place in a lightly greased 9-inch round baking pan. Cover and let rise in a warm place for 1¹/2 hours or until doubled in bulk.

Bake at 375 degrees for 12 minutes or until golden brown.

Yields 32 servings.

Sour Cream Coffee Cake

John Sullivan
Sales and Marketing
2 years

This was my aunt's recipe, and it has been popular in our family for years for holiday breakfasts.

Mix the flour, baking powder and baking soda in a medium bowl. Mix the walnuts, cinnamon and brown sugar in a small bowl.

Cream the butter and sugar in a mixer bowl until light and fluffy. Beat in the eggs 1 at a time. Stir in the sour cream and vanilla. Add the flour mixture gradually, beating well after each addition.

Pour half the batter into a greased and floured tube pan. Sprinkle with half the walnut mixture. Repeat with the remaining batter and walnut mixture.

Bake at 350 degrees for 45 minutes. Invert onto a serving plate. Sprinkle confectioners' sugar over the hot coffee cake.

Yields 12 servings.

2 cups sifted flour
1 teaspoon baking powder
$1/2$ teaspoon baking soda
$1/2$ cup chopped walnuts
1 teaspoon cinnamon
2 tablespoons brown sugar
1 cup butter or margarine, softened
$1^1/4$ cups sugar
2 eggs
1 cup sour cream
1 teaspoon vanilla extract
Confectioners' sugar

HAND-CRAFTED KNIVES SINCE 1889

CASE XX

Main Dishes

THE TWO PATTY BARRETTS

W. R. Case & Sons Cutlery Company is not what you would call a large facility. However, with 300 employees, it is possible to not know all of your fellow associates. This point was rather interestingly illustrated for us by the two Patty Barretts.

During the recipe collection phase of this book, it made sense to have a centrally located area where everyone could deposit their recipes. It was decided that the cafeteria was the perfect place. So, when Patricia L. Barrett dropped off her Breakfast Casserole recipe, she took a minute to look through the other recipes in the box. One titled Scrambled Egg Casserole caught her eye because it was so similar to hers. What really made her look twice was the name at the bottom of the form: Patricia Barrett!

Patty went to her mother-in-law, Shirley Barrett, and told her what she had discovered. Shirley then took her daughter-in-law to meet the other Patty Barrett. While the two were discussing the unbelievable coincidence of the recipes, they discovered they had even more in common. As it turns out, each of the Patty Barretts is mother to a set of fraternal twins—one boy, one girl!

Scrambled Egg Casserole

Patricia Barrett
Assembly
26 years

Brown the sausage in a skillet, stirring until crumbly; drain well and let cool. Place in a 9x13-inch glass baking dish.

Beat the eggs with the milk in a large bowl. Add the salt, dry mustard, bread and cheese and mix well. Pour over the sausage.

Cover with foil and chill overnight.

Bake, uncovered, at 350 degrees for 40 to 50 minutes or until heated through. Let stand for several minutes before serving.

Yields 8 to 10 servings.

1 pound bulk sausage
7 eggs
2 cups milk
1 teaspoon salt
1 teaspoon dry mustard
7 slices bread, torn into small
    pieces
$1^1/_2$ cups shredded sharp
    cheese

The two Patty Barretts: Patricia Barrett (standing, 26 years of service) and Patricia L. Barrett (1 year of service).

Breakfast Casserole

Patricia L. Barrett
Finishing
1 year

6 slices bread, crusts trimmed
1 (8-ounce) package shredded
   cheese
1 pound bacon
6 eggs
2 cups milk
$^1/_2$ teaspoon salt
$^1/_2$ teaspoon dry mustard

Layer the bread, cheese and bacon in a 9x13-inch baking dish.

Mix the eggs, milk, salt and dry mustard in a bowl. Pour over the layers. Chill overnight.

Bake at 325 degrees for 45 minutes.

You may add other ingredients such as green bell peppers, onions, ham or sausage to this casserole.

Yields 8 to 10 servings.

Pepper Steak

Margaret Brocious
Finishing
27 years

Mix the soy sauce, garlic and ginger in a bowl. Add the beef and toss well.

Heat the oil in a large skillet or wok. Add the beef. Cook over high heat until browned, tossing frequently. If the beef is not tender, cover and simmer for 30 minutes over low heat.

Add the green onions, red pepper and celery. Cook over high heat for 10 minutes or until the vegetables are tender-crisp, tossing frequently.

Mix the cornstarch with the water. Add to the skillet. Cook until thickened, stirring constantly. Add the tomatoes. Cook until heated through.

Serve with mashed potatoes or rice.

Yields 4 servings.

1/4 cup soy sauce
1 clove of garlic, minced
1 1/2 teaspoons grated or
    ground ginger
1 pound stir-fry steak
1/4 cup vegetable oil
1 cup thinly sliced green
    onions
1 cup 1-inch squares red or
    green bell pepper
2 ribs celery, thinly sliced
1 tablespoon cornstarch
1 cup water
2 tomatoes, cut into wedges

Southwestern Beef Brisket

Dave Frontino
Assembly
1 year

3 pounds beef brisket
1 teaspoon salt
$1/4$ teaspoon black pepper
2 tablespoons vegetable oil
$1^1/2$ cups water
1 (8-ounce) can tomato sauce
1 small onion, chopped
2 tablespoons red wine vinegar
1 tablespoon chili powder
1 teaspoon dried oregano
$3/4$ teaspoon ground cumin
$1/2$ teaspoon garlic powder
$1/8$ to $1/4$ teaspoon ground red
    pepper
$1/4$ teaspoon salt
$1/4$ teaspoon black pepper
3 medium red bell peppers, cut
    into strips
$1^1/2$ cups 1-inch carrot slices

Season the beef with 1 teaspoon salt and $1/4$ teaspoon black pepper.

Heat the oil in a Dutch oven. Add the beef. Cook until browned on both sides.

Combine the water, tomato sauce, onion, vinegar, chili powder, oregano, cumin, garlic powder, red pepper, $1/4$ teaspoon salt and $1/4$ teaspoon black pepper in a bowl and mix well. Pour over the beef.

Bake, covered, at 325 degrees for 2 hours.

Add the red peppers and carrots. Bake for 1 hour longer or until the beef is tender.

Remove the beef from the pan. Let stand for 15 minutes before slicing.

Thicken the pan drippings with a small amount of flour or cook over high heat to reduce and thicken.

The brisket may instead be wrapped in heavy-duty foil and cooked over low heat on a grill.

Yields 10 to 12 servings.

Meatball Carbonnade

Judy Mosher
Customer Repair
7 years

Cook the bacon in a medium skillet until crisp. Crumble the bacon and set aside. Do not drain the skillet.

Dissolve the bouillon cube in the boiling water.

Combine 1/4 cup of the beef bouillon, ground beef, egg, bread crumbs, 1/2 teaspoon salt and 1/8 teaspoon pepper in a bowl and mix well. Shape into small balls.

Brown the meatballs in the bacon drippings in the skillet. Remove to a 1¹/2-quart casserole.

Cook the onions in the remaining drippings in the skillet until golden brown. Spoon over the meatballs.

Stir the flour into the skillet. Add the remaining beef bouillon and the beer. Stir in the brown sugar, vinegar, 1/2 teaspoon salt, thyme and 1/8 teaspoon pepper. Cook until thickened, stirring constantly. Pour over the meatballs.

Bake, covered, at 350 degrees for 45 minutes or until the meatballs are cooked through.

Top with the parsley and crumbled bacon.

Yields 4 servings.

2 slices bacon
1 beef bouillon cube
1 cup boiling water
1 pound ground beef
1 egg, slightly beaten
1/4 cup fine dry bread crumbs
1/2 teaspoon salt
1/8 teaspoon pepper, or to taste
2 medium onions, thinly sliced
2 tablespoons flour
3/4 cup beer
1 teaspoon brown sugar
1 teaspoon vinegar
1/2 teaspoon salt
1/4 teaspoon crushed dried
    thyme
1/8 teaspoon pepper, or to taste
Chopped parsley

MEAT LOAF

Bob Baker
Assembly
4 years

2 pounds ground beef
1 onion, chopped
2 eggs
1½ cups bread crumbs
1 green bell pepper, chopped
Salt and pepper to taste
1 cup (about) catsup

Combine the ground beef, onion, eggs, bread crumbs, green pepper, salt and pepper in a bowl.

Shape into a loaf. Place in a loaf pan or shallow baking pan.

Pour the catsup over the loaf.

Bake at 400 degrees for 45 to 60 minutes or until the ground beef is cooked through.

Yields 10 servings.

CHEESY MEAT LOAF

Ed Jessup
President, Jessup and Associates
20 years

Measure and reserve 1/3 cup of the tomato sauce. Combine the remaining tomato sauce, ground beef, egg, bread crumbs, onion, salt and pepper in a large bowl and mix well.

Shape into a flat 10x12-inch rectangle on waxed paper.

Spread 1 3/4 cups of the cheese evenly over the ground beef mixture. Roll up from the short end as for a jelly roll, using the waxed paper to help. Press to seal the ends and seam. Place in a shallow baking pan.

Bake at 350 degrees for 1 hour. Drain any drippings from the pan. Pour the reserved tomato sauce over the loaf. Sprinkle with the remaining 1/4 cup cheese. Bake for 5 minutes longer.

Let stand for 10 minutes before slicing.

Yields 6 servings.

1 (15-ounce) can tomato sauce
1 1/2 pounds lean ground beef
1 egg
3/4 cup Italian bread crumbs
1/2 cup finely chopped onion
1 teaspoon salt
1/2 teaspoon pepper
2 cups shredded mozzarella cheese

CHICKEN AND DRESSING CASSEROLE

Courtney Markey
Finishing
2 years

2 packages stuffing mix
1 (10-ounce) can cream of
  chicken soup or cream of
  mushroom soup
1 cup sour cream
4 to 6 boneless chicken breast
  halves, cooked, chopped

Prepare the stuffing using the package directions. Mix the soup and sour cream in a bowl.

Layer half the soup mixture, chicken, stuffing and remaining soup mixture in a 9x13-inch baking pan.

Bake at 350 degrees for 30 to 35 minutes or until heated through.

Yields 9 servings.

Easy Chicken and Dumplings

Dolores Hatch
Accounting
31 years

Rinse the chicken. Place in a large stockpot with water to cover. Add the salt, pepper, onion and bay leaves. Bring to a boil.

Boil until the chicken pulls away from the bone. Remove the chicken and let cool.

Shred or chop the chicken, discarding the skin and bones. Remove the bay leaves from the broth.

Add the chicken soup, mushroom soup and eggs to the broth in the stockpot. Bring to a boil.

Add the lasagna noodles. Cook until the noodles are tender. Add the chopped chicken. Cook until heated through.

Yields 4 to 6 servings.

1 chicken
Salt and pepper to taste
1 onion, chopped
2 bay leaves
1 (10-ounce) can cream of
   chicken soup
1 (10-ounce) can cream of
   mushroom soup
2 hard-cooked eggs, peeled,
   chopped
1 large package lasagna
   noodles, broken into pieces

REUBEN BAKED CHICKEN

Mike Fay
Manufacturing
20 years

4 whole chicken breasts,
   deboned
1¼ teaspoons salt
1¼ teaspoons pepper
1 (16-ounce) can sauerkraut,
   drained
4 slices Swiss cheese
1 bottle Thousand Island salad
   dressing

Rinse the chicken and pat dry. Sprinkle with the salt and pepper. Place in a greased 9x13-inch glass baking dish.

Add the sauerkraut. Top with the cheese. Pour the salad dressing over the top.

Bake, covered with foil, at 325 degrees for 1½ hours.

Yields 8 servings.

Swiss Chicken

Jackie Kelly
Accounting
2 years

Rinse the chicken and pat dry. Beat the eggs and milk in a bowl. Dip chicken into the egg mixture and roll in the bread crumbs.

Heat the olive oil in a skillet. Add the chicken. Season with the salt and pepper. Sauté until lightly browned. Place in a greased casserole.

Pour the chicken broth over the chicken. Cover with the mushrooms and cheese. Sprinkle with the lemon juice.

Bake, covered, at 350 degrees for 1 hour or until the chicken is cooked through.

Yields 4 servings.

6 boneless chicken breasts
2 eggs
1 tablespoon milk
Bread crumbs
Olive oil
Salt and pepper to taste
1 cup chicken broth
1/3 pound sliced mushrooms
4 ounces Swiss cheese,
*   shredded*
Juice of 1/2 lemon

COUNTRY HAM CASSEROLE

Jeanne M. DuBois
Finishing
24 years

1 pound Velveeta cheese,
   cubed
1 cup milk
1/2 cup mayonnaise-type salad
   dressing
2 cups chopped cooked ham
1 (10-ounce) package frozen
   chopped broccoli, cooked,
   drained
5 ounces spaghetti, cooked,
   drained
1 tablespoon chopped chives

Combine the cheese, milk and salad dressing in a saucepan. Cook over low heat until the cheese is melted, stirring until smooth.

Add the ham, broccoli, spaghetti and chives and mix well. Pour into a 2-quart casserole.

Bake at 350 degrees for 35 to 40 minutes or until heated through.

Yields 6 servings.

Pork Chops Over Amber Rice

Jeanne M. DuBois
Finishing
24 years

Brown the pork chops in a nonstick skillet. Season with salt and pepper.

Place the rice in a 9x13-inch baking dish. Pour the orange juice over the rice. Arrange the pork chops over the rice. Pour the soup over the pork chops.

Bake, covered, at 350 degrees for 45 minutes. Bake, uncovered, for 10 minutes or until the pork chops are cooked through.

Yields 6 servings.

6 (3/4-inch) pork chops
Salt and pepper to taste
1 1/3 cups instant rice
1 cup orange juice
1 (10-ounce) can chicken with
    rice soup

SAUCY PORK CHOPS

Lyn Wertenberger
Accounting
6 years

6 pork chops
1 medium onion, sliced
1¼ cups catsup
1 (10-ounce) can cream of
    chicken soup
2 to 3 tablespoons
    Worcestershire sauce

I got this recipe from one of the greatest bosses I ever had. Every time I make this, I think of him.

Brown the pork chops in a nonstick skillet. Top with the onion.

Mix the catsup, soup and Worcestershire sauce in a bowl. Pour over the pork chops.

Simmer, covered, for 1 hour or until the pork chops are cooked through.

Yields 6 servings.

SPAMBURGERS

Gerald Foreman
Grinding
28 years

Grind the Spam in a food processor. Combine the Spam, catsup, vinegar, water, sugar, mustard, paprika and onion powder in a skillet and mix well.

Cook until heated through, stirring constantly.

Spoon the mixture into the buns. Butter and lightly salt the tops of the buns. Place on a baking sheet.

Bake at 350 degrees for 10 minutes or until heated through.

Yields 4 servings.

1 can Spam
$1/2$ cup catsup
2 tablespoons vinegar
$1/4$ cup water
1 tablespoon sugar
1 teaspoon prepared mustard
$1/2$ teaspoon paprika
$1/2$ teaspoon onion powder
8 hamburger buns
1 to 2 tablespoons butter
2 teaspoons salt, or to taste

VOLCANO BALLS

Kevin Pipes
Owner, Smoky Mountain Knife Works
18 years

5 pounds hot sausage

2 pounds very lean ground beef

10 to 12 ounces Colby cheese, shredded

10 to 12 ounces sharp Cheddar cheese, shredded

3 large red onions, finely chopped

6 fresh green jalapeño peppers, finely chopped

Coarsely ground black pepper to taste

Crushed red pepper to taste

Parsley flakes to taste

Garlic salt to taste

Hickory-flavored barbecue sauce

Honey-flavored barbecue sauce

Juice of 1 lemon

1/2 cup packed brown sugar

No two batches of these meatballs are ever quite the same. When grilling, be sure to cook very slowly. This is important because a really hot fire can cause the meatballs to catch fire. I know because I've done it a couple of times!

Combine the sausage and ground beef in a large bowl and mix well. Add the cheeses, onions, jalapeño peppers, black pepper, red pepper, parsley flakes and garlic salt and mix well. Shape into baseball-size balls.

Mix the barbecue sauces, lemon juice and brown sugar in a bowl. Pour enough of the sauce mixture over the meatballs to coat. Place on a grill rack.

Grill the meatballs very slowly until cooked through. Spoon the remaining sauce mixture over the meatballs and arrange in a mound. Simmer for 30 minutes over low heat.

Yields 10 to 15 servings.

HERBIE'S BAKED GOULASH

Kookie Dougherty
Assembly
27 years

My husband, Herb, is the cook in our household, and he concocted this recipe. In our town it's known as Herbie's Goulash.

Combine the macaroni, ground beef and spaghetti sauce in a bowl and mix well. Add the pepperoni, cheese, green pepper and onion and mix well.

Spoon into a roasting pan. Top with pepperoni slices.

Bake at 350 degrees for 20 minutes. Sprinkle with the cheese. Bake for 10 minutes longer.

Yields 4 to 6 servings.

1 cup macaroni, cooked, drained
1 pound ground beef, cooked, drained
1 small jar spaghetti sauce
Sliced pepperoni
Shredded mozzarella cheese
Chopped green bell pepper (optional)
Chopped onion (optional)

Marlin Schrock (left, 7 years of service) and Kookie Dougherty (27 years of service), members of the first modular manufacturing unit at W. R. Case & Sons, are working on assembling knives.

BEEF STROGANOFF

Staci Frantz
Accounting
1 year

1 quart water
1 (16-ounce) package
    fettuccini
1 cup water
1 tablespoon beef bouillon
2 tablespoons Worcestershire
    sauce
1 large onion, sliced into rings
8 ounces mushrooms, sliced
1 pound chuck steak, cut into
    $^1/_2$x1-inch pieces
2 cups sour cream

Bring 1 quart water to a boil in a 2-quart saucepan. Add the fettuccini. Cook until tender.

Bring 1 cup water, bouillon and Worcestershire sauce to a boil in a 2-quart saucepan. Add the onion, mushrooms and steak. Cook until the steak is cooked through and most of the liquid has evaporated. Stir in the sour cream.

Drain the fettuccini. Stir into the steak mixture. Serve immediately.

You may use low-sodium beef bouillon and/or low-fat or fat-free sour cream in this recipe.

Yields 4 servings.

LAZY LASAGNA

Laura Wilson
Finishing
1 year

Cook the spaghetti using the package directions. Drain and rinse in cold water.

Combine the Parmesan cheese and egg in a medium bowl. Add the spaghetti and mix well.

Mix the ground beef and spaghetti sauce in a large bowl. Stir in the onion.

Layer the spaghetti mixture, ricotta cheese and ground beef mixture in a 9x13-inch baking pan.

Bake at 350 degrees for 30 minutes. Sprinkle with the mozzarella cheese. Bake for 15 minutes longer or until the cheese is melted.

Let cool for 10 minutes before serving.

Yields 8 servings.

1 package spaghetti
$1/2$ cup grated Parmesan cheese
1 egg
1 pound ground beef, cooked, drained
1 (27-ounce) jar spaghetti sauce
1 small onion, chopped
15 ounces ricotta cheese or cottage cheese
Shredded mozzarella cheese

NOODLES À LA KING

Julie Buchanan
Etching/Engraving
20 years

12 ounces egg noodles
2 tablespoons butter
2 tablespoons chopped onion
1 (10-ounce) can cream of
    chicken soup
1 cup milk
1 (10-ounce) package frozen
    peas and carrots, thawed
2 cups chopped cooked chicken
    or turkey
1 tablespoon chopped pimento
1/4 teaspoon pepper

Cook the noodles using the package directions.

Melt the butter in a saucepan. Add the onion. Cook until tender.

Stir in the soup, milk, peas and carrots, chicken, pimento and pepper. Bring to a boil. Simmer for 15 minutes, stirring occasionally.

Drain the noodles and arrange on individual plates. Top with the sauce.

Yields 4 servings.

Russian Noodle Pudding

Jerome Fishkin
Case Board Member
1 year

This is from our Russian family members.

Combine the sour cream, cottage cheese, milk, salt, 1/8 teaspoon cinnamon and eggs in a large bowl and mix well.

Add the noodles and mix well. Pour into a buttered shallow 1¹/₂-quart baking dish. Pour the butter over the mixture. Sprinkle with the sugar.

Place the baking dish in a pan of hot water. Bake at 350 degrees for 1¹/₂ hours or until browned. Sprinkle with 1 teaspoon cinnamon.

Yields 4 servings.

1 cup sour cream
8 ounces cottage cheese
1 cup milk
¹/₂ teaspoon salt
¹/₈ teaspoon cinnamon
3 eggs, beaten
2 cups wide noodles, cooked, drained
2 tablespoons melted butter
2 tablespoons sugar
1 teaspoon cinnamon

POLISH PIEROGI

Joseph A. Lukasiewicz
Data Processing
8 years

Pierogi are a traditional Polish dish that comes in many styles. My family uses cheese, sauerkraut and potato fillings. This recipe covers the three fillings, basic noodle dough, construction of pierogi, and cooking and serving. This is one of those "labor of love" recipes that gets better each time you make it. One of the "secrets" is to roll out the noodle dough as thinly as possible without causing it to break or get holes while being filled. Prepared pierogi can be frozen and then fried as needed. Allow 4 to 6 pierogi per serving.

CHEESE FILLING

2 medium onions
1½ pounds white farmer
    cheese
1 tablespoon salt

Grate the onions with a hand grater into a fine pulp. Combine the cheese, onions and salt in a bowl and mix well.

    Cover and let stand in the refrigerator while you prepare the noodle shells.

Yields enough for 30 pierogi.

SAUERKRAUT FILLING

14 ounces canned or fresh
    mushrooms, drained
2 medium onions, chopped
1 (1-quart) jar sauerkraut,
    drained

Brown the mushrooms and onions in a large skillet. Add the sauerkraut. Cook until the sauerkraut is heated through, stirring frequently.

    Remove from the heat and let stand while you prepare the noodle shells.

Yields enough for 30+ pierogi.

Potato Filling

This appears to be a "clean the fridge" type of filling. The egg appears to "bind" the other materials together.

Brown the onions in a large skillet. Combine the onions, mashed potatoes, parsley, egg and salt in a bowl and mix well. Let stand while you prepare the noodle shells.

Yields enough for 30 pierogi.

2 medium onions, chopped
4 cups cold mashed potatoes
1 tablespoon parsley
1 egg
1 teaspoon salt

Kluski Egg Noodles

Place the flour in a large bowl in the shape of a bird's nest. Sprinkle the salt evenly over the flour. Add the eggs to the inside of the "nest." Stir until the flour and eggs form a "gooey" yellow ball.

Roll the dough to the thickness of a quarter on a floured board, sprinkling with additional flour if needed. Cut into circular "shells" using a 3^1/$_2$- to 4-inch cookie cutter or the top from an old coffeepot, being careful not to make any holes in the shells. Reshape any remaining dough into a ball. Roll and cut as directed above. Continue making circles until all the dough is used.

Yields 25 to 30 shells.

3 cups flour
1 teaspoon salt
6 eggs

continued on next page

CREATION OF PIEROGI

This process can get rather sloppy, so choose a work area away from where you rolled out the dough (you may need to make more dough). Fill a small bowl with water. Hold 1 dough shell in the center of your palm. Place 1 heaping teaspoonful of 1 of the fillings in the center of the shell. Dip 1 finger of your free hand into the water and "paint" $1/2$ of the exposed circle edge. Stretch the dough carefully without making any holes and fold in half, joining the "painted" rim of the circle with the unpainted. The dough should form a half circle. Pinch the edges to seal the filling inside the dough. Sprinkle lightly with flour and place on a waxed paper-lined baking sheet. Continue until you use all the filling or the dough shells.

PREPARATION OF PIEROGI

Fill a large pot with cold water and a dash of salt. Bring to a rolling boil. Add the pierogi approximately 12 at a time to keep them from splitting. Boil for 12 minutes. The pierogi will float; and, if there are no holes in the dough and they were sealed, the filling will be locked inside. Remove to a rack or a waxed paper-lined baking sheet to dry.

COOKING AND SERVING PIEROGI

Fry the pierogi (and onions, if you like) in butter in a large skillet. Turn when the dough is becoming golden brown. Only the parts of the pierogi that actually touch the skillet will brown. Serve as a side dish or main dish. Serve with sour cream if you like.

Pasta Louie

Helen G. Johnson
Finishing
24 years

Melt the butter in a saucepan. Add the garlic powder, chick-peas, tomato, green pepper and Parmesan cheese and mix well.

Cook until heated but not cooked through. Add the pasta, sausage and bacon and mix well.

Spoon into a 9x12-inch baking pan. Sprinkle with the mozzarella cheese.

Bake at 350 degrees for 30 minutes.

Yields 6 servings.

1/2 cup butter
Garlic powder to taste
1 can chick-peas
1 tomato, chopped
1 green bell pepper, chopped
1/2 cup grated Parmesan cheese
1 package spiral pasta, cooked, drained
1 1/2 pounds Italian sausage, cooked
8 ounces bacon, crisp-fried, crumbled
1 pound mozzarella cheese, shredded

Members of the honing department are from left: Margaret Brocious (27 years of service), Helen Johnson (24 years of service), and Cliff Mott (33 years of service).

HAND-CRAFTED KNIVES SINCE 1889

CASE XX

RIGATONI RHONI

Rhoni McGraw
Assembly
1 year

1 (16-ounce) package rigatoni
1 pound ground round
1 large onion, chopped
3 tomatoes, chopped
4 cups sour cream
Shredded mozzarella cheese

This is a self-conjured recipe.

Boil the rigatoni in a saucepan for 10 minutes or until tender. Drain, rinse and set aside. Brown the ground round with the onion in a skillet, stirring frequently; drain and set aside.

Combine the tomatoes, sour cream, rigatoni and ground round mixture in a large bowl and mix well. Pour into a 9x13-inch glass baking dish. Top with the cheese.

Bake at 350 degrees for 30 minutes.

Serve with Texas toast.

Yields 6 servings.

BARBECUE SAUCE

Dave Frontino
Assembly
1 year

3 cups catsup
2 cups packed dark brown
  sugar
1/4 cup Worcestershire sauce
3/4 cup peach schnapps

Combine the catsup, brown sugar, Worcestershire sauce and schnapps in a saucepan.

Bring to a boil and reduce the heat. Simmer until the mixture is heated through and the flavors have blended.

Yields 12 to 15 servings.

Old-Time Hot Dog Sauce

Dianna Lewis
Data Processing
23 years

Brown the ground beef with the onion in a large skillet over medium heat, stirring until the ground beef is crumbly; drain well.

Add the tomato sauce, chili powder and Worcestershire sauce. Bring to a boil and reduce the heat. Simmer for 10 minutes. Season with the oregano.

Yields 10 servings.

8 ounces ground beef
1 medium onion, chopped
1 (8-ounce) can tomato sauce
1 tablespoon chili powder
$1/2$ teaspoon Worcestershire sauce
$1/8$ teaspoon oregano, or to taste

Homemade Spaghetti Sauce

Mike Baker
Operations Manager
7 years

Combine the water, tomatoes, tomato paste, sugar, oregano, cheese, salt and hot sauce in a 1-gallon kettle. Bring to a boil. Boil for 2 hours, stirring occasionally.

Add the tomato sauce. Boil for 1 hour; reduce the heat. Simmer for 3 hours.

Yields 12 servings.

3 quarts water
1 (24-ounce) can crushed tomatoes
1 (4-ounce) can tomato paste
2 tablespoons sugar
$1/4$ cup ground oregano
$1/4$ cup grated Parmesan cheese
$1/4$ cup salt
2 tablespoons red hot sauce
1 (16-ounce) can tomato sauce

VEGETABLES
&
SIDE DISHES

BAKED BEANS

Karen Troutman
Data Processing
22 years

1 (16-ounce) package dried
    navy, Great Northern or
    tiny lima beans
6 cups water
4 to 8 ounces bacon, chopped
1/2 cup chopped onion
1/2 cup catsup, or to taste
1/2 cup packed brown sugar
1 teaspoon salt, or to taste
1 teaspoon dry mustard

Sort and rinse the beans. Combine with the water in a large stockpot. Cook until slightly soft.

Add the bacon, onion, catsup, brown sugar, salt and mustard and mix well. Pour into a small roasting pan.

Bake at 300 to 325 degrees for 3 to 4 hours or until the beans are of the desired consistency, adding additional water if needed.

Yields 8 to 10 servings.

BEAN CASSEROLE

Christopher Keller
Sales and Marketing
3 years

This recipe was given to me by my oldest sister, Mary Kay Cucuzza.

Brown the ground beef with the onion in a skillet, stirring until the ground beef is crumbly; drain well. Season with the salt and pepper. Add the brown sugar, pork and beans and barbecue sauce. Cook until bubbly and heated through. Remove to a 9-inch round glass baking dish.

Cut each biscuit into halves to form half circles. Arrange cut side down around the edge of the baking dish. Sprinkle with the cheese.

Bake at 375 degrees for 25 to 30 minutes or until the biscuits are golden brown.

Yields 4 servings.

1 pound ground beef
1 medium onion, chopped, or
  to taste
Salt and pepper to taste
2 tablespoons brown sugar
1 (28-ounce) can pork and
  beans
1 cup barbecue sauce
1 (10-count) can buttermilk
  biscuits
1 cup shredded Cheddar cheese

BLOCK PARTY BEANS

Nancy Fox
Finishing
5 years

2 pounds ground beef
2 cups chopped onions
1 cup chopped celery
1 (10-ounce) can tomato soup
1 (6-ounce) can tomato sauce
1/2 cup catsup
1 (16-ounce) can green beans,
    drained
1 (17-ounce) can lima beans,
    drained
1 (16-ounce) can chili beans
1 (16-ounce) can pork and
    beans
1/2 cup packed brown sugar
2 tablespoons prepared
    mustard

This is excellent for family reunions or other parties.

Brown the ground beef in a large Dutch oven over medium heat, stirring until crumbly; drain well. Add the onions and celery. Cook until tender.

Stir in the soup, tomato sauce and catsup. Simmer for 15 minutes. Spoon into a large kettle or roaster. Add the green beans, lima beans, undrained chili beans, undrained pork and beans, brown sugar and mustard and mix well.

Bake at 350 degrees for 1 hour.

Yields 25 servings.

Calico Beans

Frank F. Mason
Finishing
5 years

Cook the bacon in a large skillet until crisp. Drain on paper towels.

Brown the ground beef in the bacon drippings in the skillet, stirring until crumbly; drain well. Add the onion. Sauté until tender.

Combine the ground beef mixture, catsup, salt, brown sugar, mustard and vinegar in a bowl and mix well. Add the beans, stirring gently just until mixed. Spoon into a 3-quart baking dish. Sprinkle with the bacon.

Bake at 350 degrees for 40 minutes.

Yields 8 servings.

6 slices bacon
8 ounces ground beef
1 onion, chopped
1/2 cup catsup
1 teaspoon salt
3/4 cup packed brown sugar
1 teaspoon dry mustard
2 teaspoons vinegar
1 (16-ounce) can kidney
    beans, partially drained
1 (16-ounce) can pork and
    beans, partially drained
1 (16-ounce) can lima beans or
    butter beans, partially
    drained

GRANDMA'S BEANS

Rick Whelan
Finishing
5 years

1 pound dried beans
1/8 teaspoon baking soda
8 ounces salt pork
1/4 cup sugar
1/2 (1-pound) package brown
　　sugar
Molasses to taste
Salt and pepper to taste

Sort the beans. Soak the beans in water to cover overnight. Drain and rinse.

Combine the beans with water to cover in a large stockpot. Add the baking soda. Boil for 10 minutes. Drain and rinse.

Combine the beans and salt pork in a large stockpot. Add enough water to cover. Cook until the beans are tender. Add the sugar, brown sugar, molasses, salt and pepper. Spoon into a baking dish.

Bake at 350 degrees for 1 hour.

The beans will thicken as they cool.

Yields 8 to 10 servings.

Carla Hervatin (Finishing, 1 year of service) and Rick Whelan (Finishing, 5 years of service) are loading knives onto the racks of the parts washer.

GREEN BEAN CASSEROLE

Julie Buchanan
Etching/Engraving
20 years

Combine the green beans, soup, milk and onions in a bowl. Season with salt and pepper. Spoon into a baking dish.

Bake at 350 degrees for 30 minutes.

Serve immediately.

Yields 4 servings.

2 cans green beans, drained
1 (10-ounce) can cream of
    mushroom soup
3/4 cup milk
1 cup French-fried onions
Salt and pepper to taste

BROCCOLI STIR-FRY

Donna Whitford
Blanking
30 years

1 bunch broccoli
3 tablespoons vegetable oil
2 tablespoons soy sauce
1 teaspoon cornstarch
1 tablespoon honey
$1/2$ teaspoon ginger
$1/4$ teaspoon hot pepper sauce
$1/4$ cup slivered almonds

My Hawaiian daughter-in-law made this for us. Now I make it for my family, and they enjoy it very much.

Rinse the broccoli and cut off the florets. Peel the stems and cut into $1/4$-inch slices.

Heat the oil in a large skillet. Add the broccoli. Stir-fry for 5 minutes or until tender-crisp.

Mix the soy sauce and cornstarch in a small bowl. Add the honey, ginger and hot pepper sauce and mix well. Pour over the broccoli.

Cook until the sauce is slightly thickened. Stir in the almonds.

Yields 4 servings.

CASE XX

BROCCOLI AND CHEESE QUICHE

Cathy McCleary
Human Resources
15 years

You may alter this recipe to suit your tastes by omitting the onion or green pepper, by using a different cheese or even by adding bacon bits.

Drain the broccoli and squeeze out the excess moisture.

Combine with the skim milk, cheese, onion, green pepper, eggs, salt and pepper in a bowl and mix well. Pour into a buttered 9-inch pie plate.

Bake at 340 degrees for 30 to 35 minutes or until set.

Yields 6 to 8 servings.

1 package frozen broccoli, thawed
1¼ cups skim milk
1¼ cups shredded Cheddar cheese
1 small onion, chopped
1 green bell pepper, chopped
6 eggs
Salt and pepper to taste

CARROT SWEET POTATO T'SIMMES

Jerome Fishkin
Case Board Member
1 year

2 or 3 large carrots, thinly
    sliced
¹/₂ cup water
¹/₂ teaspoon salt
2 large sweet potatoes, thinly
    sliced
1 tart apple, cored, thinly
    sliced
¹/₄ cup honey
2 to 3 teaspoons apricot
    marmalade

This 150-year-old recipe comes from our European family members.

Combine the carrots, water and salt in a 2-quart saucepan. Simmer, covered, until the carrots are tender, adding additional water if needed.

Add the sweet potatoes and apple. Simmer for 25 minutes or until the sweet potatoes are tender, adding additional water if needed.

Add the honey and marmalade. Simmer until the mixture is heated through and the flavors have blended.

Serve hot or cold.

Yields 5 servings.

CORN PUDDING

Richard Brandon
Environmental/Safety Manager
7 years

Combine the corn, milk, 2 tablespoons flour, 1/4 cup sugar, baking powder, eggs and salt in a bowl and mix well. Pour into a 9x13-inch baking dish.

Bake at 325 degrees for 40 minutes or until the top is slightly hardened.

Combine the butter, water, 1/2 cup sugar and 2 tablespoons flour in a saucepan. Boil until thickened, stirring frequently. Pour over the baked mixture.

Yields 6 servings.

2 cans cream-style corn
1 cup milk
2 tablespoons flour
1/4 cup sugar
1 teaspoon baking powder
2 eggs
1/8 teaspoon salt, or to taste
1/2 cup butter
1/2 cup water
1/2 cup sugar
2 tablespoons flour

HAND·CRAFTED·KNIVES·SINCE·1889

CASE XX

BAKED POTATO FRIES

Karen Stebbins
Hafting
7 years

4 medium russet potatoes, cut
    into large wedges
1 tablespoon vegetable oil
1/4 teaspoon freshly ground
    pepper
1/8 teaspoon salt
2 cloves of garlic, minced
    (optional)

Combine the potatoes with cold water to cover in a large bowl. Let stand for 15 minutes.

Drain the potatoes in a colander. Spread between double layers of paper towels. Press down to dry the potatoes. Transfer to a large bowl.

Sprinkle the potatoes with the oil, pepper and salt. Arrange in a single layer on a baking sheet sprayed with nonstick cooking spray.

Bake at 425 degrees for 20 minutes. Turn the potatoes and sprinkle with the garlic. Bake for 20 minutes longer.

Yields 4 servings.

Hash Brown Casserole

Randy Gourley
Hafting
5 years

This recipe came from West Virginia.

Pour 1 cup of the margarine over the potatoes in a large bowl.

Mix the soup and sour cream in a medium bowl. Stir into the potatoes. Add the onion and cheese and mix well. Pour into a 9x13-inch baking dish. Top with the crumbs. Pour the remaining 1/4 cup margarine over the top.

Bake at 350 degrees for 45 minutes.

Yields 8 servings.

1 1/4 cups melted margarine
1 (2-pound) package frozen hash brown potatoes, thawed
1 (10-ounce) can cream of chicken soup
2 cups sour cream
1/2 cup chopped onion
2 cups shredded Cheddar cheese
2 cups butter cracker crumbs

Vegetable Medley Casserole

Robin Walker
Etching/Engraving
23 years

Combine the vegetables and soup in a bowl and mix well. Spoon into a large casserole. Dot with the butter.

Bake at 350 degrees for 35 minutes. Top with the cheese and pepperoni. Bake for 7 to 10 minutes longer or until the cheese is melted.

Yields 8 to 10 servings.

2 packages frozen broccoli, carrots and cauliflower
2 (10-ounce) cans cream of mushroom soup
1 tablespoon (about) butter
1 cup shredded mozzarella cheese
1 cup chopped pepperoni

Lib's Sweet Potato Casserole

Randy Travis
Case Collector

3 cups mashed cooked sweet
   potatoes
1 cup sugar
2 eggs
1 teaspoon vanilla extract
$1/3$ cup milk
$1/2$ cup butter or margarine,
   softened
1 cup packed brown sugar
$1/3$ cup flour
$1/3$ cup butter or margarine
1 cup finely chopped pecans

Combine the sweet potatoes, sugar, eggs, vanilla, milk and $1/2$ cup butter in a mixer bowl. Beat until smooth. Spoon into a greased shallow 2-quart casserole.

Combine the brown sugar, flour, $1/3$ cup butter and pecans in a bowl and mix well. Sprinkle over the sweet potato mixture.

Bake at 350 degrees for 30 minutes.

Yields 8 to 10 servings.

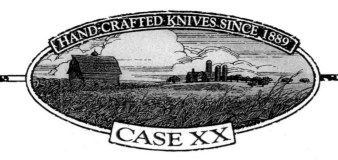

Baked Macaroni and Cheese

Gail Reid
Customer Service
7 years

Cook the macaroni to the desired degree of doneness using the package directions; drain well.

Spray the bottom of an 8x11-inch baking pan with nonstick cooking spray. Alternate layers of the macaroni, cheese and margarine in the pan until all the ingredients are used. Pour the milk over the top.

Bake at 350 degrees for 2 hours or until golden brown.

Yields 15 servings.

2 pounds macaroni
4 pounds extra-sharp Cheddar
   cheese, shredded
1/2 cup margarine
1 cup milk

FRANKFURTER CORN BREAD

Bobbea Southard
Finishing
5 years

¹/₂ cup chopped celery
1 cup chopped onion
¹/₂ cup chopped green bell
pepper
¹/₄ cup vegetable oil
2¹/₂ cups canned tomatoes
8 frankfurters, cut into eighths
¹/₂ teaspoon salt (optional)
1 (11-ounce) package corn
muffin mix

Sauté the celery, onion and green pepper in the oil in a skillet until the onion is browned. Remove from the heat.

Add the tomatoes, frankfurters and salt and mix well. Pour into a greased 2¹/₂-quart casserole.

Prepare the corn muffin mix using the package directions. Pour over the frankfurter mixture. Garnish with additional small frankfurter slices.

Bake at 375 degrees for 35 minutes.

Yields 6 to 8 servings.

Fiesta Rice Casserole

Donna Whitford
Blanking
30 years

I first tasted this in Arizona. A Mexican friend of my daughter-in-law gave me the recipe.

Combine the rice, olives and green pepper in a bowl, stirring to mix. Spoon into a buttered 2-quart casserole.

Sauté the onion in the butter in a skillet until lightly browned. Add the beef broth, chili powder, cinnamon, cumin, oregano and salt and mix well. Simmer for 5 minutes. Pour over the rice mixture.

Bake, covered, at 375 degrees for 25 minutes or until heated through.

Mix the avocado with the lemon juice in a small bowl, stirring to coat well. Remove the avocado and stir the lemon juice into the baked mixture. Arrange the avocado and tomato wedges over the top.

Yields 10 servings.

$3^1/2$ cups cooked rice
1 (2-ounce) can sliced black
    olives, drained
$1/2$ green bell pepper, chopped
$1/2$ cup chopped onion
1 tablespoon butter or
    margarine
$3/4$ cup beef broth
$1^1/2$ teaspoons chili powder
$1/4$ teaspoon ground cinnamon
$1/4$ teaspoon ground cumin
$1/4$ teaspoon oregano
$1/2$ teaspoon salt
1 avocado, peeled, sliced
2 tablespoons lemon juice
2 medium tomatoes, peeled,
    cut into wedges

HAND·CRAFTED KNIVES·SINCE·1889

CASE XX

DESSERTS

APPLE PUDDING CAKE

Tom Arrowsmith
Manufacturing Manager
1 year

1 cup sugar
1¼ cups flour
1 teaspoon baking soda
1 teaspoon cinnamon
½ teaspoon cloves
3 tablespoons butter, softened
2 tablespoons cold water
1 teaspoon vanilla extract
2 cups chopped apples
2 tablespoons (heaping)
    cornstarch
1 cup packed brown sugar
1 cup hot water
1 tablespoon butter
1 tablespoon vanilla extract
⅛ teaspoon salt, or to taste

This is a favorite family recipe.

Combine the sugar, flour, baking soda, cinnamon and cloves in a bowl and mix well. Add 3 tablespoons butter, the cold water and 1 teaspoon vanilla and mix well. Stir in the apples. The batter will be thick. Pour into a nonstick 9x11-inch cake pan.

Bake at 350 degrees for 30 minutes. Cut into pieces.

Combine the cornstarch, brown sugar, hot water, 1 tablespoon butter, 1 tablespoon vanilla and salt in a saucepan. Cook until thickened, stirring frequently.

Spoon over each piece when serving.

Yields 8 servings.

BLUEBERRY TEA CAKE

Lyn Wertenberger
Accounting
6 years

I received this recipe from a family friend over 35 years ago, and it is still one of my favorite desserts.

Sift 2 cups flour, the baking powder and salt together.

Cream $1/4$ cup margarine and $3/4$ cup sugar in a mixer bowl until light and fluffy. Beat in the egg and milk. Add the flour mixture gradually, beating well after each addition. Fold in the blueberries. Spread in a greased and floured 9x11-inch cake pan.

Mix $1/2$ cup sugar, $1/4$ cup flour and the cinnamon in a bowl. Cut in $1/4$ cup margarine until crumbly. Sprinkle over the cake batter.

Bake at 375 degrees for 40 to 45 minutes.

Yields 10 to 12 servings.

2 cups flour
2 teaspoons baking powder
$1/4$ teaspoon salt
$1/4$ cup margarine, softened
$3/4$ cup sugar
1 egg
$1/2$ cup milk
2 cups blueberries
$1/2$ cup sugar
$1/4$ cup flour
$1/2$ teaspoon cinnamon
$1/4$ cup margarine

Coconut Cake

Calvin Abrams
Shipping
26 years

1 (2-layer) package yellow
    cake mix
1 (4-ounce) package vanilla
    instant pudding mix
1^1/3 cups water
4 eggs
^{1}/4 cup vegetable oil
2 cups flaked coconut
1 cup chopped walnuts or
    pecans
^{1}/4 teaspoon coconut extract
1 recipe white frosting
^{1}/2 cup toasted flaked coconut

Combine the cake mix, pudding mix, water, eggs and oil in a large bowl and mix well. Stir in 2 cups coconut and the walnuts. Pour into 3 greased and floured 9-inch cake pans.

Bake at 350 degrees for 35 minutes. Cool in the pans for several minutes. Remove to a wire rack to cool completely.

Beat the flavoring into the frosting. Spread between the layers and over the top and side of the cake. Sprinkle with ^{1}/2 cup coconut.

Yields 16 servings.

CREAMSICLE CAKE

Mark Stormer
Maintenance
24 years

My wife got this recipe from her supervisor at Zippo.

Prepare and bake the cake mix using the package directions for a 9x13-inch cake pan. Pierce the cake numerous times.

Combine 1 package gelatin and the hot water in a bowl and mix well. Pour over the cake. Chill thoroughly.

Combine the remaining gelatin, the pudding mix, milk, whipped topping and vanilla in a bowl and mix well. Spread over the cake.

Yields 12 servings.

1 (2-layer) package orange cake mix
1 (3-ounce) package orange gelatin
1 cup hot water
1 cup cold water
1 (3-ounce) package orange gelatin
1 (4-ounce) package vanilla instant pudding mix
1 cup milk
8 ounces whipped topping
1 teaspoon vanilla extract

Pina Colada Cake

Shirley Boser
Sales and Marketing
21 years

1/3 cup 80-proof dark rum
1 (4-ounce) package coconut
   instant pudding mix
1 (2-layer) package white cake
   mix
4 eggs
1/2 cup water
1/4 cup vegetable oil
1 (8-ounce) can crushed
   pineapple
1 (4-ounce) package coconut
   cream instant pudding mix
1/3 cup 80-proof dark rum
8 ounces whipped topping
1 cup flaked coconut

*My aunt, Grace Gordon of Randolph, New York,
gave me this recipe. It is as great as she is.*

Combine 1/3 cup rum, coconut pudding mix,
cake mix, eggs, water and oil in a large
mixer bowl. Beat at medium speed for 4
minutes. Pour into 2 greased and floured 9-inch
cake pans.

Bake at 350 degrees for 25 to 30 minutes or
until the layers spring back when lightly
touched; do not underbake. Cool in the pans for
15 minutes. Remove to a wire rack to cool
completely.

Combine the undrained pineapple, coconut
cream pudding mix and 1/3 cup rum in a bowl
and beat well. Fold in the whipped topping.
Spread between the layers and over the top and
side of the cake. Sprinkle with the coconut.

Yields 12 servings.

SWEDISH CHRISTMAS CAKE

Beth Soble
Accounting
18 years

Combine the water, salt and oats in a saucepan. Boil for 1 minute. Let cool.

Combine 1/2 cup margarine, sugar, 1 cup brown sugar, eggs, flour, cinnamon and baking soda in a large bowl and mix well. Stir in 1 1/2 cups pecans. Pour into a greased 9x13-inch cake pan.

Mix 1/2 cup margarine, 3/4 cup brown sugar, 1 1/2 cups pecans and vanilla in a bowl. Sprinkle over the cake batter.

Bake at 350 degrees for 45 minutes.

Yields 15 servings.

2 cups water
2 teaspoons salt
1 cup rolled oats
1/2 cup margarine, softened
1 cup sugar
1 cup packed brown sugar
2 eggs
1 1/2 cups flour
1 teaspoon cinnamon
1 teaspoon baking soda
1 1/2 cups chopped pecans or
  walnuts
1/2 cup margarine
3/4 cup packed brown sugar
1 1/2 cups chopped pecans or
  walnuts
1 teaspoon vanilla extract

WACKY CAKE

Michael J. DuBois
Hafting
22 years

1¹/₂ cups flour
1 cup sugar
3 tablespoons baking cocoa
1 teaspoon baking soda
¹/₂ teaspoon salt
5 tablespoons melted butter
1 teaspoon vinegar
1 teaspoon vanilla extract
1 cup warm water

Sift the flour, sugar, cocoa, baking soda and salt into a large bowl.

Add the butter, vinegar, vanilla and warm water and mix well. Pour into a nonstick 8x8-inch cake pan.

Bake at 350 degrees for 25 to 30 minutes or until the cake tests done.

Yields 8 to 12 servings.

WHISKEY CAKE

Stacey Holly
Finishing
1 year

Combine the pudding mix, cake mix, eggs, sour cream, whiskey, milk and oil in a large bowl and mix well.

Layer the cake batter and walnuts 1/2 at a time in a greased bundt pan. Stir gently with a spoon several times.

Bake at 350 degrees for 1 hour.

Yields 12 to 15 servings.

1 (4-ounce) package vanilla
   instant pudding mix
1 (2-layer) package yellow
   cake mix
5 eggs, beaten
2 tablespoons sour cream
1/2 cup whiskey
1/2 cup milk
3/4 cup vegetable oil
1 cup chopped walnuts

Whoopie Cake

Ken DuBois
Maintenance
27 years

3 cups flour
2 teaspoons baking soda
2 cups sugar
1 cup baking cocoa
2 eggs
1 cup sour milk
1 cup hot water
2 teaspoons vanilla extract
1 cup shortening
2 egg whites
2 tablespoons vanilla extract
1/4 cup flour
1 (1-pound) package
   confectioners' sugar

Combine 3 cups flour, baking soda, sugar, cocoa, eggs, sour milk, hot water and 2 teaspoons vanilla in a bowl and mix well. Pour into a nonstick 11x17-inch cake pan.

Bake at 350 degrees for 15 to 20 minutes. Let cool.

Combine the shortening, egg whites, 2 tablespoons vanilla and 1/4 cup flour in a bowl and mix well. Add the confectioners' sugar gradually, beating well after each addition until of a spreading consistency.

Spread the filling over 1 baked layer. Top with the other baked layer. Spread with the remaining filling.

Yields 18 to 24 servings.

Yum Yum Gems

Linda Huntington
Finishing
7 years

My grandmother would make these for my uncles and grandfather during hunting season.

Cream the shortening, brown sugar and egg in a mixer bowl until light and fluffy.

Add the cinnamon, nutmeg, cloves, sour milk and baking soda and mix well.

Stir in the dates and pecans. Add the flour and mix well.

Fill paper-lined muffin cups 2/3 full with the batter.

Bake at 375 degrees for 45 minutes.

Yields 12 to 15 servings.

$1/2$ cup shortening
1 cup packed brown sugar
1 egg
1 teaspoon cinnamon
1 teaspoon nutmeg
1 teaspoon cloves
1 cup sour milk
1 teaspoon baking soda
Chopped dates to taste
Chopped pecans or walnuts to
    taste
2 cups flour

CREAMY FROSTING

Erma Spaulding
Finishing
27 years

1 (3-ounce) package instant
  pudding mix, any flavor
1 envelope whipped topping
  mix
1 cup milk

Combine the pudding mix, whipped topping mix and milk in a mixer bowl. Beat until smooth and creamy.

Yields 1¹/₂ to 2 cups.

Larry Saar (28 years of service) weighs components from the bunks that will later be used in the assembly of Case knives.

QUICK CARAMEL FROSTING

Vicki Geer
Grinding
1 year

My grandmother would make this to top her mayon-naise cake for dessert with Sunday dinners.

Combine the butter, brown sugar and milk in a saucepan. Cook until the butter is melted and the brown sugar is dissolved, stirring frequently. Bring to a rapid boil. Boil for 1 minute. Remove from the heat.

Add the confectioners' sugar gradually, beating constantly until the mixture loses its gloss.

Yields 2¹/₂ to 3 cups.

6 tablespoons butter
³/₄ cup packed brown sugar
6 tablespoons milk
2 cups confectioners' sugar

JUBILEES

Linda Cranmer
Grinding
23 years

2³/₄ cups flour
¹/₂ teaspoon baking soda
1 teaspoon salt
¹/₂ cup shortening
1 cup packed brown sugar
¹/₂ cup sugar
2 eggs
1 cup evaporated milk
1 teaspoon vanilla extract
1 cup chopped walnuts
2 tablespoons butter
2 cups sifted confectioners'
　　sugar
¹/₄ cup sweetened condensed
　　milk

Sift the flour, baking soda and salt together. Combine the shortening, brown sugar, sugar and eggs in a bowl and mix well. Stir in the evaporated milk and vanilla. Add the flour mixture gradually, mixing well after each addition. Stir in the walnuts.

Chill for 1 hour. Drop by rounded teaspoonfuls 2 inches apart onto a greased cookie sheet.

Bake at 350 degrees for 10 minutes.

Heat the butter in a saucepan until golden brown. Beat in the confectioners' sugar and condensed milk gradually, beating until smooth. Spread over the warm cookies.

Yields 4 dozen.

LEMON ZUCCHINI DROP COOKIES

Barbara Seeley
Blanking
1 year

My dear friend Millie gave me this recipe.

Mix the flour, baking powder and salt together.

Cream the margarine and sugar in a mixer bowl until light and fluffy. Beat in the egg and lemon peel. Add the flour mixture gradually, beating until a smooth dough forms. Stir in the zucchini and walnuts.

Drop by teaspoonfuls onto a nonstick cookie sheet.

Bake at 350 degrees for 15 to 17 minutes or until lightly browned.

Yields 5 dozen.

2 cups flour
1 teaspoon baking powder
1/2 teaspoon salt
3/4 cup margarine, softened
3/4 cup sugar
1 egg, beaten
1 1/2 teaspoons grated lemon peel
1 cup shredded unpeeled zucchini
1 cup chopped walnuts

PECAN BUTTER BALLS

Sherry Southard
Customer Service
23 years

2 cups sifted flour
1/4 cup sugar
1/2 teaspoon salt
1 cup butter, softened
2 teaspoons vanilla extract
2 cups chopped pecans or
   walnuts
1/4 to 1/2 cup confectioners'
   sugar

I usually make these for the Christmas holidays.

Combine the flour, sugar, salt, butter and vanilla in a bowl and mix well. Stir in the pecans.

Shape into 1-inch balls. Place on a nonstick cookie sheet.

Bake at 325 degrees until lightly browned. Let cool. Roll in the confectioners' sugar.

Yields 2 to 3 dozen.

Peanut Butter Fingers

Barbara Henderson
Customer Service
6 years

Cream the butter, sugar and brown sugar in a mixer bowl until light and fluffy. Blend in the egg, $^1/_3$ cup peanut butter, baking soda, salt and vanilla. Add the flour and oats and mix well. Spread in a greased 9x13-inch baking pan.

Bake at 350 degrees for 20 to 25 minutes or until lightly browned.

Sprinkle immediately with the chocolate chips. Let stand until the chocolate is melted. Spread the chocolate over the top.

Combine the confectioners' sugar and $^1/_4$ cup peanut butter in a bowl. Add enough of the milk to make of a thin consistency, mixing well. Drizzle over the chocolate.

Let cool and cut into bars.

Yields 4 dozen.

$^1/_2$ cup butter, softened
$^1/_2$ cup sugar
$^1/_2$ cup packed brown sugar
1 egg
$^1/_3$ cup peanut butter
$^1/_2$ teaspoon baking soda
$^1/_4$ teaspoon salt
$^1/_2$ teaspoon vanilla extract
1 cup flour
1 cup quick-cooking oats
1 cup chocolate chips
$^1/_2$ cup sifted confectioners'
    sugar
$^1/_4$ cup peanut butter
2 to 4 tablespoons milk

Peanut Butter Scotcharoos

Marilyn Skillman
Etching/Engraving
7 years

2 cups light corn syrup
2 cups sugar
3 cups peanut butter
10 cups crisp rice cereal
2 cups chocolate chips
2 cups butterscotch chips

Heat the corn syrup and sugar in a saucepan, stirring until the sugar is dissolved. Blend in the peanut butter. Add the cereal and mix well. Press into a greased 9x13-inch baking pan.

Melt the chocolate chips and butterscotch chips in a double boiler over hot water. Spread over the cereal mixture.

Chill until the chocolate mixture hardens. Cut into squares.

Yields 1¹/₂ dozen.

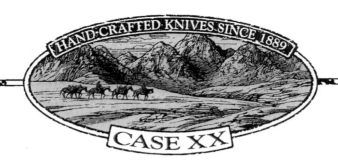

YOLANDA COOKIES

Sabatina Lombardi
Assembly
30 years

This is a traditional Italian cookie.

Beat the eggs in a large bowl. Add the sugar, shortening, lemon extract, 1 teaspoon vanilla, salt and baking powder and mix well. Add the flour gradually, mixing well after each addition until a smooth dough forms.

Roll 1 teaspoon of the dough at a time on a lightly floured surface. Place on a nonstick cookie sheet.

Bake at 350 degrees until set; do not overbake.

Mix the confectioners' sugar, margarine and 1 teaspoon vanilla in a bowl. Stir in enough milk to make of a spreading consistency. Spread over the cooled cookies.

Yields 7 dozen.

6 eggs
1 cup sugar
1 cup melted shortening
1 teaspoon lemon extract
1 teaspoon vanilla extract
1/2 teaspoon salt
2 tablespoons baking powder
4 to 5 cups flour
1 (1-pound) package
   confectioners' sugar
1 teaspoon margarine,
   softened
1 teaspoon vanilla extract
1/4 cup (about) milk

HAND-CRAFTED KNIVES SINCE 1889

CASE XX

Swedish Apple Pie

Dot Colley
Finishing
22 years

1 cup sour cream
2 tablespoons flour
³/₄ cup sugar
1 egg
¹/₈ teaspoon salt, or to taste
1 teaspoon vanilla extract
2 cups cooked sliced apples
1 unbaked (10-inch) pie shell
³/₄ cup packed brown sugar
¹/₃ cup margarine
1 cup flour
1 teaspoon cinnamon

Given to me by my aunt, this recipe won a blue ribbon in 1988 at a local grocery store pie contest.

Beat the sour cream, 2 tablespoons flour, sugar, egg, salt and vanilla in a mixer bowl until stiff. Fold into the apples in a large bowl. Pour into the pie shell.

Bake at 350 degrees for 45 minutes.

Combine the brown sugar, margarine, 1 cup flour and cinnamon in a bowl, mixing until crumbly. Sprinkle over the pie. Bake for 20 minutes longer.

Yields 8 servings.

Another grinder, another machine… Mike Colley (26 years of service) works on trays of blades by putting them through the front edging machine.

FAVORITE CHERRY PIE

Joette Tripodi
Assistant to the President
1 year

This is my mother's recipe. It is one of my favorites, a treat for friends who claim they don't like cherry pie. Everyone loves this!

Pour the pie filling into the pie shell. Bake at 375 degrees for 30 minutes.

Mix the eggs, sugar, margarine, lemon juice, vanilla and coconut in a bowl. Pour over the pie filling.

Bake for 20 to 25 minutes longer or until the topping is slightly browned.

Yields 8 servings.

1 can cherry pie filling
1 unbaked pie shell
2 eggs, beaten
$1/2$ cup sugar
$1/4$ cup melted margarine
2 teaspoons lemon juice
$1/4$ teaspoon vanilla extract
$1/2$ cup flaked coconut

Ricotta Pies

Rosa Vigliotta
Blanking
8 years

3 cups flour
4 eggs
^{1}/2 cup sugar
2 teaspoons baking powder
^{1}/2 cup margarine
8 eggs
2 teaspoons vanilla extract
2 pounds ricotta cheese
^{1}/2 cup sugar

Traditional Italian dish usually served at Easter. It resembles cheesecake.

Combine the flour, 4 eggs, ^{1}/2 cup sugar, baking powder and margarine in a bowl and mix well. Press into 2 lightly greased 9-inch pie plates.

Mix 8 eggs and vanilla in a bowl. Add the cheese and ^{1}/2 cup sugar and mix well. Pour into the pie shells.

Bake at 300 degrees for 1 hour.

Yields 16 servings.

CHOCOLATE PIES

Sharon Hollebeke
Purchasing
2 years

Combine the sugar, cornstarch and salt in a large saucepan. Add the milk gradually, stirring until mixed. Add the cocoa and oil. Cook until the mixture boils and thickens, stirring constantly. Boil for 1 minute. Remove from the heat.

Stir a small amount of the hot mixture into the egg yolks; stir the egg yolks into the hot mixture. Beat in the vanilla. Pour into the pie shells.

Bake at 400 degrees for 20 minutes or until the edges of the pie shells are lightly browned. Let stand to cool. Spread with the whipped topping.

Yield: 12 to 16 servings.

3 cups sugar
2/3 cup cornstarch
1/2 teaspoon salt
6 cups milk
3/4 cup baking cocoa
1/4 cup vegetable oil
4 egg yolks, beaten
1 teaspoon vanilla extract
2 unbaked pie shells
16 ounces whipped topping

CHOCOLATE PEANUT BUTTER PIE

Steve Kellogg
Shipping
1 year

2 (4-ounce) packages chocolate
    pudding mix
$1/2$ cup peanut butter
1 graham cracker pie shell
Whipped topping

Prepare the pudding mix using the package directions. Stir in the peanut butter while the mixture is cooking.

Pour into the pie shell. Chill until set.

Serve with the whipped topping.

Yields 6 to 8 servings.

German Sweet Chocolate Pie

Randy Reid
Owner, Shepherd Hills Walnut
23 years

Combine the chocolate and butter in a saucepan. Cook over low heat until melted, stirring until blended. Remove from the heat. Blend in the evaporated milk gradually.

Mix the sugar, cornstarch and salt in a bowl. Beat in the eggs and vanilla. Add the chocolate mixture gradually, blending well after each addition. Pour into the pie shell. Sprinkle with a mixture of the coconut and pecans.

Bake at 375 degrees for 45 to 50 minutes or until puffed and browned. Cover loosely with foil during the last 15 minutes of baking time if the crust browns too quickly. Cool for 4 hours or longer before cutting.

Chill until serving time.

Yields 8 servings.

4 ounces German's sweet chocolate
1/4 cup butter or margarine
1 2/3 cups evaporated milk
1 1/2 cups sugar
3 tablespoons cornstarch
1/8 teaspoon salt
2 eggs
1 teaspoon vanilla extract
1 unbaked fluted (9-inch) pie shell
1 1/3 cups flaked coconut
1/2 cup chopped pecans

TASSIES

Bunny Comilla
Human Resources Manager
3 years

3 ounces cream cheese,
   softened
$1/2$ cup margarine, softened
1 cup flour
Finely chopped walnuts to
   taste
$1^1/2$ cups packed brown sugar
2 tablespoons melted butter
2 eggs
1 teaspoon vanilla extract
$1/8$ teaspoon salt, or to taste

*This recipe is in memory of my grandmother, Rose
Anderson.*

Combine the cream cheese, margarine and
flour in a bowl and mix well. Shape into 24
small balls. Pat the balls onto the bottom and
side of a tassie pan. Sprinkle lightly with the
walnuts.

Combine the brown sugar, butter, eggs,
vanilla and salt in a bowl and beat well. Pour
into the prepared pan.

Bake at 350 degrees for 30 minutes.

Yields 6 to 8 servings.

EASY PIE CRUST

Jerry Prosser
Finishing
5 years

Combine the flour and salt in a medium bowl. Cut in the shortening until crumbly. Sprinkle in the water 1 tablespoon at a time, tossing with a fork until the mixture forms a ball.

Press into the shape of a 5- to 6-inch pancake. Roll on a lightly floured surface. Trim to 1 inch larger than an inverted pie plate. Loosen carefully.

Fold into quarters and place in the pie plate. Unfold and press into place. Fold the edge under. Prick several times and flute the edge.

When preparing a 1-crust pie, prebake the pie shell at 350 degrees for 6 to 10 minutes or until lightly browned.

Yields 1 pie shell.

1¹/₃ cups flour
¹/₂ teaspoon salt
¹/₂ cup shortening
3 tablespoons cold water

Perfect Apple Crisp

Jerry Prosser
Finishing
5 years

4 cups sliced peeled apples
$^1/_2$ cup flour
$^1/_2$ cup rolled oats
$^3/_4$ teaspoon cinnamon
$^3/_4$ teaspoon nutmeg
$^2/_3$ to $^3/_4$ cup packed brown
    sugar

Layer the apples in a greased 8x8-inch or 8x10-inch baking pan.

Combine the flour, oats, cinnamon, nutmeg and brown sugar in a bowl, stirring until crumbly. Sprinkle over the apples.

Bake at 375 degrees for 30 minutes or until the topping is browned and the apples are tender.

You may prepare this in a glass casserole and microwave on High for 12 minutes.

Yields 8 to 10 servings.

PEACH COBBLER DESSERT

Lyn Wertenberger
Accounting
6 years

This is an old family favorite.

Arrange the peaches in a baking pan. Mix 2/3 cup sugar, 2 tablespoons flour and cinnamon in a bowl. Sprinkle over the peaches. Dot with the butter.

Combine 1 cup flour, 2 tablespoons sugar, baking powder and salt in a bowl and mix well. Add the shortening, milk and egg and mix well. Drop by spoonfuls over the peaches.

Bake at 350 degrees for 25 to 30 minutes or until lightly browned and heated through.

Yields 6 to 8 servings.

3 cups canned peaches
2/3 cup sugar
2 tablespoons flour
1/2 teaspoon cinnamon
1 tablespoon (about) butter
1 cup flour
2 tablespoons sugar
1 1/2 teaspoons baking powder
1/2 teaspoon salt
1/3 cup shortening
3 tablespoons milk
1 egg

OLD-FASHIONED RHUBARB PUDDING

Lisa Patry
Customer Service
1 year

1¹/2 cups hot water
3 cups chopped rhubarb
¹/2 cup tapioca
1¹/4 cups sugar
¹/2 teaspoon salt
Cinnamon to taste

Elderly friends gave me this recipe, which has been passed down through their family.

Combine the hot water, rhubarb and tapioca in a double boiler. Cook over hot water for 15 minutes or until the tapioca is clear, stirring frequently.

Add the sugar and salt. Cook for several minutes, stirring until the sugar is dissolved. Sprinkle with cinnamon. Chill thoroughly.

Serve with a dollop of whipped cream or vanilla ice cream.

Yields 4 servings.

KEARNEY'S KREME BRULEE

Barbara W. Kearney
Case Board Member
1 year

Beat the eggs and egg yolks in a bowl. Bring the whipping cream, milk and sugar almost to a boil in a heavy saucepan. Whisk a small amount of the hot mixture into the eggs; whisk the eggs into the hot mixture.

Cook over moderate heat for 3 to 4 minutes or until the custard coats a spoon, stirring constantly. Remove from the heat. Stir in the vanilla.

Pour into 6 custard dishes or a 9-inch shallow baking dish. Set the dishes in a large pan and place in the oven. Pour hot water into the outer pan level with the custard.

Bake at 300 degrees for 35 to 45 minutes or until the center of the custard is set. Remove from the water bath and cool. Cover and chill thoroughly.

Sift the brown sugar evenly over the custard, spreading to the edge. Broil as close to the heat source as possible for $1^{1}/_{2}$ minutes or until browned but not burned. Chill until serving time.

Yields 6 servings.

3 eggs
3 egg yolks
$2^{1}/_{3}$ cups whipping cream
$^{2}/_{3}$ cup milk
$^{1}/_{4}$ cup sugar
1 teaspoon vanilla extract
$^{3}/_{4}$ cup packed light brown
    sugar

CHEESECAKE PIE

Martha Coverston
Accounting
2 years

3/4 cup sugar
16 ounces cream cheese,
  softened
3 eggs
1 cup sour cream
3 tablespoons sugar
1 teaspoon vanilla extract

This is a delicious, easy cheesecake without a crust.

Cream 3/4 cup sugar, the cream cheese and eggs in a mixer bowl until light and fluffy. Pour into a lightly buttered 9-inch pie plate.

Bake at 350 degrees for 30 minutes. Remove from the oven and let cool for 20 minutes.

Mix the sour cream, 3 tablespoons sugar and vanilla in a bowl. Spread over the filling.

Bake for 10 minutes. Let cool. Chill thoroughly.

Yields 8 servings.

CHOCOLATE DELIGHT

Nancy Bacha
Finishing
26 years

Butter a 9x13-inch dish and line with some of the whole graham crackers.

Prepare the pudding mix using the package directions, using 1/4 cup less milk than directed. Blend in the whipped topping.

Layer the pudding and remaining graham crackers 1/2 at a time over the graham crackers in the dish, ending with graham crackers.

Combine the chocolate, corn syrup, vanilla, butter, confectioners' sugar and milk in a bowl. Mix until of a spreading consistency. Spread over the graham crackers.

Chill for 48 hours before serving.

Yields 12 to 15 servings.

1 package graham crackers
2 (4-ounce) packages French
   vanilla pudding mix
9 ounces whipped topping
2 envelopes pre-melted or
   liquid chocolate
2 tablespoons light corn syrup
1 tablespoon vanilla extract
3 tablespoons melted butter
1/2 cup confectioners' sugar
3 tablespoons milk

CREAM PUFF DESSERT

Sharon DuBois
Blanking
22 years

1 cup water
¹/₂ cup margarine
1 cup flour
4 eggs
8 ounces cream cheese,
   softened
3 (4-ounce) packages vanilla
   instant pudding mix
4 cups milk
12 ounces whipped topping
Chocolate syrup to taste

Bring the water and margarine to a boil in a saucepan. Add the flour and mix well. Cool for 2 minutes. Beat in the eggs 1 at a time with a mixer. Pour into a greased 9x13-inch baking pan.

Bake at 400 degrees for 30 to 35 minutes or until browned. Let cool.

Beat the cream cheese in a mixer bowl. Add the pudding mix and milk gradually, beating well after each addition. Pour into the cooled crust.

Spread with the whipped topping. Drizzle with the chocolate syrup.

Chill until serving time.

Yields 12 to 15 servings.

FRUIT PUDDING

Leonard Larson
Finishing
32 years

My mother made this for holidays.

Prepare the pudding mix using the package directions. Blend in the whipped topping.

Add the fruit cocktail, cherries, mandarin oranges and pineapple and mix well. Stir in the bananas, marshmallows and walnuts.

Chill until serving time.

Yields 10 servings.

1 (6-ounce) package vanilla
   instant pudding mix
8 ounces whipped topping
1 (16-ounce) can fruit cocktail,
   drained
1 jar maraschino cherries,
   drained
1 large can mandarin oranges,
   drained
1 (16-ounce) can pineapple,
   drained
2 bananas, sliced
1 (10-ounce) package flavored
   marshmallows
Chopped walnuts (optional)

Punch Bowl Cake

Randy Gourley
Hafting
5 years

1 (2-layer) package yellow
  cake mix
2 (4-ounce) packages vanilla
  instant pudding mix
1 large can crushed pineapple,
  drained
5 bananas, sliced
2 (10-ounce) packages frozen
  strawberries, thawed
16 ounces whipped topping

This very good recipe came from York, South Carolina. Blueberry pie filling may be used instead of the strawberries.

Prepare the cake mix using the package directions. Bake half the batter in a nonstick 8-inch cake pan and half in a 9-inch cake pan.

Prepare the pudding mix using the package directions.

Place the smaller cake layer in a punch bowl. Spread with half the pudding, pineapple, bananas, strawberries and whipped topping. Repeat the layers, using the larger cake layer.

Chill until serving time.

Yields 24 servings.

PEANUT BUTTER FUDGE

Dot Hazzard
Blanking
30 years

Combine the confectioners' sugar, butter and evaporated milk in a large heavy saucepan.

Cook over medium heat until the confectioners' sugar is dissolved and the butter is melted, stirring constantly. Cook to 234 to 240 degrees on a candy thermometer, soft-ball stage, stirring constantly.

Remove from the heat. Stir in the marshmallow creme and peanut butter quickly. Pour into a lightly greased 9x13-inch pan.

Let stand until set. Cut into pieces.

Yields 5 pounds.

2 (1-pound) packages
   confectioners' sugar
1/2 cup butter or margarine
1 (13-ounce) can evaporated
   milk
1 (7-ounce) jar marshmallow
   creme
1 (18-ounce) jar peanut butter

HAND-CRAFTED KNIVES SINCE 1889

CASE XX

FROM OUR RETIREES

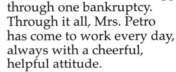

A MOST EXTRAORDINARY PERSON

At fourteen, having just graduated from St. Bernard's parochial school, Mary Petro was looking for a summer job. She began work at Case July 1, 1924. She retired July 1, 1994.

During those seventy years, the company has moved several times, has had five different owners, and has struggled through one bankruptcy. Through it all, Mrs. Petro has come to work every day, always with a cheerful, helpful attitude.

At her emotional retirement party, Mrs. Petro said, "It's been a joy working here. It seems like yesterday that I was hired. I will miss everybody and it will be hard for me to leave."

In his tribute to Mrs. Petro, Case President George Brinkley told the other employees that she "leaves a legacy to all of us that transcends the workplace. Loyalty, dedication, devotion to duty, trust—these are all examples that serve us well not just in our jobs but in our lives."

Shortly after Mr. Brinkley's arrival at Case in 1991, he offered the manufacturing employees the opportunity to work ten-hour shifts, four days a week. Concerned about Mrs. Petro's ability to work two additional hours a day, he went to ask her about it.

He recounted her response. "I was told—in no uncertain terms—that Mary could work just as long and just as

effectively as anybody in the factory. I promptly said, 'Yes, ma'am,' and went about my business. And she was right."

Mr. Brinkley continued: "In making my rounds each morning, Mary was always one of my favorite stops. She never complained but was not afraid to tell me if something was wrong. She was always positive in her attitude and genuinely proud of her job."

In recognition of her contributions and longevity, Case issued a limited edition knife bearing her name, with a portion of the proceeds going to Mrs. Petro and the American Cancer Society, her favorite charity.

Appropriately, the last knife Mrs. Petro wrapped was placed in a plaque and given to Gina Snyder, Case's newest employee.

Both Mrs. Petro and her mother, who worked for Case for more than fifty years, are pictured on the back cover of this book.

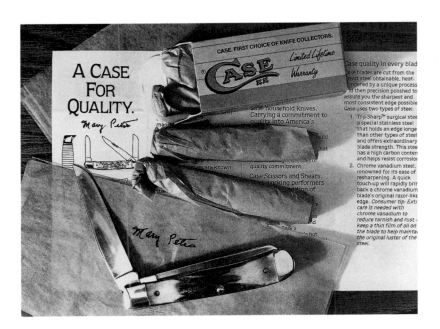

LIME GELATIN SALAD

Mary Petro
Retired 1994
70 years

20 marshmallows, or 4 ounces
1 cup milk
1 small package lime gelatin
6 ounces cream cheese,
    softened
2 (8-ounce) cans crushed
    pineapple
2 cups whipped cream or
    whipped topping

Combine the marshmallows and milk in a double boiler. Cook until the marshmallows are melted, stirring frequently.

Pour over the gelatin in a bowl, stirring until the gelatin is dissolved. Add the cream cheese, beating until smooth. Stir in the pineapple. Let cool.

Fold in the whipped cream. Pour into a serving dish. Chill until set.

Yields 8 to 10 servings.

OATMEAL CAKE

Mary Petro
Retired 1994
70 years

Mix the flour, baking soda, baking powder, salt and cinnamon together.

Pour the water over the oats in a large bowl. Let cool. Add 1 cup brown sugar, sugar, margarine and eggs and mix well. Add the flour mixture gradually, mixing well after each addition. Pour into a nonstick 9x13-inch cake pan.

Bake at 350 degrees for 40 to 45 minutes or until the cake tests done.

Mix 1 cup brown sugar, butter and milk in a saucepan. Bring to a boil. Boil for 2 minutes. Remove from the heat. Stir in the pecans and coconut. Spread over the cake.

Yields 12 to 15 servings.

$1^{1}/_{2}$ cups flour
1 teaspoon baking soda
$^{1}/_{2}$ teaspoon baking powder
$^{1}/_{2}$ teaspoon salt
1 teaspoon cinnamon
$1^{1}/_{2}$ cups boiling water
1 cup quick-cooking oats
1 cup packed brown sugar
1 cup sugar
$^{1}/_{2}$ cup margarine or
    shortening
2 eggs, beaten
1 cup packed brown sugar
1 tablespoon butter
$^{1}/_{4}$ cup milk
1 cup chopped pecans or
    walnuts
1 cup coconut

CRY BABIES

Fred Burns
Retired 1981
22¹/₂ years

1 cup sugar
1 cup butter or margarine,
    softened
2 eggs
1 cup dark molasses
2 teaspoons ginger
2 teaspoons cinnamon
2 teaspoons baking soda
1 cup hot strong coffee
1 teaspoon vinegar
¹/₈ teaspoon salt, or to taste
4¹/₂ cups flour

This was my wife's grandmother's recipe. She always had a plateful whenever anyone dropped in to visit.

Combine the sugar, butter, eggs, molasses, ginger and cinnamon in a large bowl and mix well.

Dissolve the baking soda in the coffee. Stir in the vinegar and salt.

Add the flour and coffee mixture alternately to the molasses mixture, mixing well after each addition.

Drop by spoonfuls onto a nonstick cookie sheet.

Bake at 350 degrees for 10 minutes. Cool on a wire rack.

Yields 3 dozen.

HAND-CRAFTED KNIVES SINCE 1889

CASE XX

BEEF CASSEROLE

Ted Johnson
Retired 1988
41 1/2 years

My aunt gave me this recipe many years ago. It's nice for families or for church dinners.

Drain the peas, reserving the liquid. Brown the ground beef in a skillet, stirring until crumbly and drain well.

Layer the potatoes, carrots, peas, onions and celery in a 2 1/2-quart casserole. Top with the ground beef.

Mix the reserved liquid with the soup in a bowl. Pour over the ground beef.

Bake at 350 degrees for 1 to 2 hours or until the mixture is heated through and the vegetables are tender.

Yields 8 servings.

2 cans peas
1 pound ground beef
2 medium potatoes, peeled, sliced
2 carrots, sliced
3 onions, sliced
1 rib celery, sliced
1 (10-ounce) can tomato soup

EASTER EGGS BREAD

John Lombardi
Retired 1988
34 years

1 package dry yeast
2/3 cup warm milk
6 eggs
1 cup sugar
5 tablespoons melted
    shortening
2 teaspoons lemon extract
8 cups (or more) flour

Dissolve the yeast in the warm milk. Beat the eggs in a large bowl. Add the sugar and mix well.

Stir in the yeast mixture. Add the shortening and mix well. Stir in the flavoring. Add the flour gradually, mixing well after each addition until a soft dough forms. Cover and let rise in a warm place until doubled in bulk.

Punch the dough down and shape into loaves. Place in 2 greased 8-inch loaf pans and 2 greased 6-inch loaf pans. Let stand in a warm place until 1 inch above top of pans.

Bake at 325 to 350 degrees for 40 to 45 minutes or until lightly browned.

Yields 36 to 40 servings.

Broccoli Bake

Lois Pessia
Retired 1996
21 years

Cook the broccoli using the package directions, omitting the salt; drain well.

Combine the soup, cheese and egg in a large bowl and mix well. Blend in the mayonnaise and milk. Stir in the broccoli. Pour into a 6x10-inch baking dish. Cover and chill until baking time.

Mix the butter and bread crumbs in a small bowl. Cover and chill until baking time.

Sprinkle the bread crumbs over the broccoli mixture.

Bake at 375 degrees for 30 to 35 minutes or until the bread crumbs are browned.

Yields 4 to 6 servings.

1 (10-ounce) package frozen
  cut broccoli
1 (10-ounce) can cream of
  mushroom soup
$1/2$ cup shredded sharp cheese
1 egg, beaten
$1/4$ cup mayonnaise or
  mayonnaise-type salad
  dressing
$1/4$ cup milk
1 tablespoon melted butter or
  margarine
$1/4$ cup fine dry bread crumbs

HARVEY WALLBANGER CAKE

Lois Pessia
Retired 1996
21 years

1 (2-layer) package yellow
   cake mix
1 (4-ounce) package vanilla
   instant pudding mix
$1/2$ cup melted shortening
4 eggs
$1/4$ cup vodka
$1/4$ cup galliano
$3/4$ cup orange juice
Confectioners' sugar
Softened butter
Lemon juice or orange juice

Combine the cake mix, pudding mix, shortening, eggs, vodka, galliano and $3/4$ cup orange juice in a mixer bowl. Beat for 4 minutes. Pour into a greased and lightly floured bundt pan.

Bake at 350 degrees for 45 to 50 minutes or until the cake tests done. Let stand until cool. Invert onto a cake plate. Drizzle with a glaze of confectioners' sugar, butter and lemon juice or just sprinkle with confectioners' sugar.

Yields 16 servings.

HAND-CRAFTED KNIVES SINCE 1889

CASE XX

INDEX

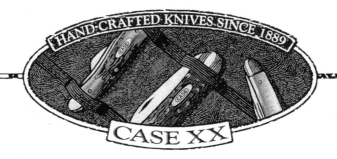

HAND-CRAFTED KNIVES SINCE 1889
CASE XX

INDEX

HAND-CRAFTED KNIVES SINCE 1889

CASE XX

Index

ANATOMY OF A CASE KNIFE

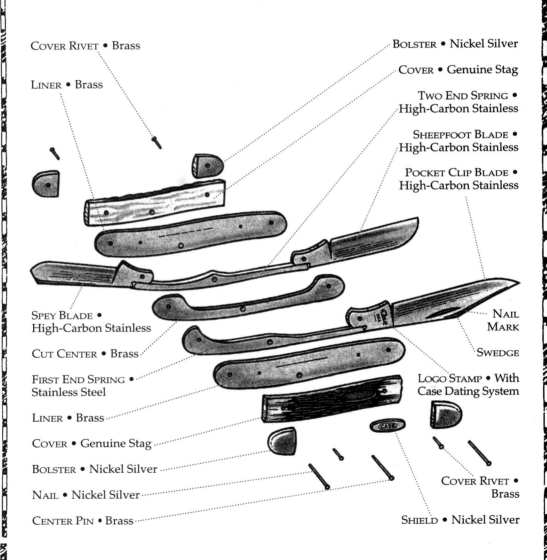

COVER RIVET • Brass

LINER • Brass

BOLSTER • Nickel Silver

COVER • Genuine Stag

TWO END SPRING •
High-Carbon Stainless

SHEEPFOOT BLADE •
High-Carbon Stainless

POCKET CLIP BLADE •
High-Carbon Stainless

SPEY BLADE •
High-Carbon Stainless

CUT CENTER • Brass

FIRST END SPRING •
Stainless Steel

LINER • Brass

COVER • Genuine Stag

BOLSTER • Nickel Silver

NAIL • Nickel Silver

CENTER PIN • Brass

NAIL MARK

SWEDGE

LOGO STAMP • With
Case Dating System

COVER RIVET •
Brass

SHIELD • Nickel Silver

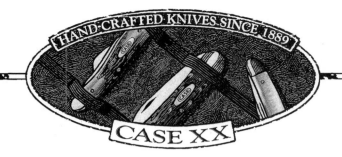

Order Form

W. R. Case & Sons Cookbook and Historical Companion

Mail order to:

W. R. Case & Sons Cutlery Company
Owens Way
Bradford, Pennsylvania 16701
Attention: Joette Tripodi

Please send _____ copies of the *W. R. Case & Sons Cookbook and Historical Companion*. (Florida and Pennsylvania residents add applicable sales tax.)

Price per book $19.95 _____

Postage and handling per book $ 4.00 _____

Sales tax _____

Total amount enclosed _____

Make checks payable to: W. R. Case & Sons Cutlery Company

Credit cards accepted: ☐ VISA ☐ MasterCard

Credit card number: ☐☐☐☐☐☐☐☐☐☐☐☐☐☐☐☐☐☐☐☐

Expiration: ___ - ___ - ___   Signature _____

Name: _____

Address: _____

City / State / Zip: _____

Phone number: _____

Are you a member of the Case Collectors Club? ___ yes ___ no

Would you like membership information? ___ yes ___ no

W.R. CASE & SONS CUTLERY CO.